Presented to the

Ironside Memorial Library

by

Alumni

Rev. & Mrs.
Leslie Napier

CHRISTIAN WORSHIP

CHRISTIAN WORSHIP

AN INTRODUCTORY OUTLINE

BY

T. S. GARRETT

Second edition

LONDON
OXFORD UNIVERSITY PRESS
NEW YORK   TORONTO

Oxford University Press, Ely House, London, W.1

GLASGOW NEW YORK TORONTO MELBOURNE WELLINGTON
CAPE TOWN SALISBURY IBADAN NAIROBI LUSAKA ADDIS ABABA
BOMBAY CALCUTTA MADRAS KARACHI LAHORE DACCA
KUALA LUMPUR HONG KONG

First published 1961
Second edition 1963
Reprinted 1966

Printed in Great Britain

PREFACE

THIS BOOK is written unashamedly with a bias which derives from the author's life in the Church of South India. It has grown out of lectures delivered to Indian theological students and was originally intended to be a text-book for them, as well as other Indian readers. In consequence the worship of the Church in India, past and present, may appear to the western reader to be given an undue prominence.

Several readers of the manuscript suggested that it contained material which might be useful to readers outside India and the author agreed with the Oxford University Press to tone down or omit some of the local colour before publication. This has in some measure been done; but second thoughts prompted the reflection that readers in other countries would do well to pay more attention to the liturgical tradition of the Syrian Christians of Kerala, and that the liturgical developments of the past twenty years in the Churches of the Reformation established in India were among the most significant in the Church of today. Much that could have been omitted has therefore been retained, with the consent of the publishers.

South India has also inspired the ecumenical tendency of the book. The contemporary revival of worship marches significantly with the ecumenical movement. It may well be that this revival is doomed to ultimate frustration unless church union finds fulfilment; for we cannot hope for fullness of worship except in the fullness of communion with our brethren now separated from us.

Perhaps this bias will give interest enough to compensate for the volume's manifest slenderness in liturgical scholarship and its obvious dependence on the researches of others, to whom a debt of gratitude must be expressed. The author is also most thankful for the criticisms and suggestions of many friends whose names are too numerous to mention.

T. S. GARRETT

Tirumaraiyur,
  November 1959.

30766

CONTENTS

CONTENTS

CHAPTER 1

THE MEANING OF WORSHIP

WORSHIP IN THE CHURCH TODAY

THE Church of the mid-twentieth century is a Church in movement. It is probably true to say that its pilgrimage from established tradition to a new understanding of its nature and mission is at least as transforming as the pilgrimage to which it was called at the time of the Reformation. Of all the aspects of this change in the Church's life the movement towards unity, which we call 'the ecumenical movement', is undoubtedly of most far-reaching significance. If it is true, as we believe it to be, that worship is the life-blood of the Church, the present-day efforts towards reform of worship (often called 'liturgical movements') are among the most important activities of the ecumenical movement. Indeed the Faith and Order Commission of the World Council of Churches has the study of worship and of trends towards its revision as one of its chief concerns. Alongside and often in close touch with the liturgical studies of the non-Roman Churches stand the great liturgical congresses and the schools of eminent liturgists in the Roman Church.

It is not surprising, then, that new books on worship figure prominently in our Church bookshops. Some of them are the fruits of research by liturgical scholars; others endeavour to give a simpler and briefer presentation of the findings of these more technical studies. In a third group, and perhaps most important for the Christian minister and layman who want to know how the worship of their own congregations can be improved, are those books which view worship from a pastoral point of view and seek to apply the work of the liturgists to the public services of the congregation. Equally important for our study are the many revised service books which our generation has seen. When we come to the modern period our attention will be especially directed to these. A common characteristic which we shall expect to find in most modern books about worship is a dissatisfaction with worship as it has been, whether 'Catholic' or 'Protestant', and either a desire for reform or a justification of reform already in process of being achieved. In fact these books belong to the liturgical movements, either that of the Roman Church (whose movement has some claim to be called *the* Liturgical movement) or those of other Churches closely or remotely connected with the Roman movement. When we hear of Roman or Anglican priests celebrating the Eucharist facing the people across a simple wooden communion table with their congregation grouped closely around them, or of 'folk masses' in which the musical setting of the people's parts is derived from popular contemporary music; when we come across valiant attempts by protestant ministers to do away with the 'ministerial monologue' in their services and to inspire their people to take an effective part; when we learn of communities like that of Iona off the coast of Scotland or Christian ashrams[1] in India, which are seeking to bring worship into a closer relation with the whole of life, we are coming into contact with this revival of worship the influence of which is spread throughout the world-wide Church.

This revival, though it is in part a transition from the old to the new, must not indulge merely in a search for novelty. Rather it must be concerned with a return to the beginning. We must ask what the Church of the New Testament meant by worship and what the worship of previous centuries has to contribute to our discovery of the true nature of man's dedica-

---

[1] An *ashram* in the Hindu classics is a company of disciples living with a religious teacher or *guru*. In modern parlance it has been used to denote a variety of communities devoted to religious or social service.

tion of himself to God in adoration and offering. The remainder of this first chapter seeks to answer the question : 'What is the meaning of worship?' But in examining worship apart from its historical development we can only give a preliminary answer as a guide to further study. A fuller answer can only be attained after we have asked how Christians have actually worshipped through the ages. That is why the greater part of this book is devoted to a historical outline of the great liturgical traditions of Christendom. Only after we have learnt something of the background in the past of the worship which we know and take part in in the present, shall we be able, as we tentatively try to do in the last chapter, to apply our knowledge to the betterment of worship in our own Church's life.

GOD'S PURPOSE THAT MEN SHOULD WORSHIP

Christian teaching at its highest has always proclaimed with united voice that man exists for the glory of God. In a world which tends to judge all human activity by its economic usefulness and which values the Church largely for its contribution to social welfare, this needs to be asserted emphatically. It is one of the points at which God's judgment on the world's scale of values is made known. Even Christians who reject Marx's economic view of man are often prone to this false view of human life.

This does not, of course, mean that acts of charity and service to our neighbours are less important than private or public acts of worship. Nothing could be further from the outlook of the New Testament than to suppose this. We do, however, need to put Christian social action in its right perspective and to view it as undertaken to the praise and glory of God—as an act of worship in fact—rather than as something to be valued only for its usefulness to man. Perhaps our Lord's parable of the sheep and the goats may help us to understand the nature of service to our fellow men and its relation to faith and worship. Loving service is of value in God's sight and receives its eternal reward; but the point of the parable would seem to be that the 'sheep' are in one respect as spiritually blind as the 'goats' who have done nothing for their neighbours. They have failed to see that their humanitarian activities were done unto Christ and are, therefore, part of the purpose for which they were created, the glory of God.

FORMS OF WORSHIP

Worship, then, embraces the whole of life; for it is our response to a God who is everywhere present and active in his universe. But, as the Bible makes clear to us, God who is everywhere has also willed to reveal himself at particular times and in particular situations to people of his choice. So too, though the whole of life may for the dedicated soul provide the material of worship, there are, none the less, times when we must say with Jacob at Bethel, 'Surely God is in *this* place'.

It appears to be part of man's nature as soul-in-body that this should be so. He is specially aware of God's presence at his appointed hours of prayer and places of worship. He uses in his approach to God ritual and ceremonial (prescribed forms of words and actions).[1] He gives dramatic form to his worship in sacrifice and sacrament.

But what happens when these outward actions of worship cease to be inspired by the living religious experience with which they began? It is a sign of man's fallen nature that there is always a danger of this happening. When we meet with an ancient traditional form of worship still in use we may well ask : is it like a fossil, or can it be compared to a

[1] The words 'rite' and 'ceremony' are often used loosely and interchangeably. The main emphasis, however, in 'rite' and 'ritual' is on the form of words, though not excluding the actions. 'Ceremony' and 'ceremonial' refer to outward actions, but ones which are normally accompanied by forms of words.

torch? If it is completely divorced from any religious experience and is just an old custom, then it is a 'fossil', an empty, lifeless relic from the past. But many old forms of worship still do inspire devotion in the hearts of worshippers who participate in them. They convey to those same worshippers the knowledge of God from former times and inspire a like faith in the present time. Then they are 'torches' by which the heritage of heavenly light is passed on from generation to generation.

When worship has become incurably fossilized, and when, as a result, religion is divorced from morality, God in his mercy and judgement sends forth his Spirit on a prophetic movement which may express itself in revolt against the traditional forms of worship and in many cases try to dispense with set forms altogether. We see this illustrated in the Old Testament by the eighth-century prophets who denounced sacrifice, though their aim may have been to purify it rather than abolish it. In the history of the Church the Reformation is a classical example. Even those reformers who retained the ancient ways of worship all radically revised them in doing so; and there are Christian groups, of whom the best known are the Society of Friends (Quakers), who assert that the outward and visible forms of sacrament are unnecessary. Their only form of public worship is the common meeting, much or all of which may be spent in silent waiting for the light of Christ in the soul; though in their family worship prayers and carefully chosen passages of scripture find a prescribed place.[1]

We must not undervalue the Quaker way of worship both as a means of nurturing the participant in spiritual growth and as a prophetic witness to the essential inwardness of all true worship. There will doubtless always be those whose inclinations prompt them to approach God in worship with

[1] See *Ways of Worship* (S.C.M. Press, 1951), pp. 169-74. This book is a valuable quarry of information about numerous heritages of worship. (See also pp. 182-3 for a select bibliography, where place and date of publication will be found, when not given in footnotes.)

but 'the thinnest human veil between'—to use Browning's phrase. All the same, we must insist that the broader stream of the Church's adoration is in accordance with man's bodily nature as God has created him. We are always using conventional signs in the common intercourse of life. We cannot demonstrate or maintain friendship, for instance, without handshakes and hospitality in the form of food and drink. Our life is daily enriched by the symbols of art and music. These are the ways in which our invisible personalities find expression in and through the material bodies with which they are inextricably linked. So too in the fullness of Christian worship there must be shape and colour, sound and action as beautiful and full of meaning as man, inspired by the Spirit of God, can make it; for these visible things are part of God's creation for man's use and his own glory. If we are to accept the pictures in the Book of Revelation of the worship of heaven, that too will not be without the splendour of colour, music, and symbolic action.

WORSHIP IN FELLOWSHIP

Further, there is the fact that religion as a whole and worship in particular, both in their primitive beginnings and their maturest development, have never been something an individual can do in isolation from his fellows. To describe religion as 'the flight of the alone to the alone' is, to say the least, one-sided. Fresh development in worship may begin with the vision of the seer and saint; but if that vision is to alter the course of human life, it must be passed on to the community at large through some corporate religious activity. The significance, for instance, of the story of Jacob at Bethel in Genesis 28 is that it is regarded as the history of the foundation of a centre of worship which has survived until the writer's own day. The communion of Moses with God in his vision of the burning bush sends him back to his own people with the mission to lead them forth to 'worship God on this mountain'. Above all, he who was to tread the path of Calvary alone says to his followers on the previous night, 'Do this in remembrance of me'. So too, in the life of the Church, the inspiration of individual men and women of vision has led to new depth in corporate worship : the many founders of religious orders in medieval Europe, the leaders of the Christian ashram movement in India and Ceylon, the newly-formed religious communities in the Reformed Church of France.

THE DISTINCTIVENESS OF CHRISTIAN WORSHIP

Dr. J. A. T. Robinson, in his books *In the End, God* and *The Body,* has pointed out that, according to the biblical view, the human body is the symbol not of man's individuality, but of his solidarity. 'It is the bond of continuity and unity between man and his environment, between individual and community, between generation and generation.' Our bodily nature, therefore, may be regarded as the justification, not only for the outward symbolism of worship, as we have noted above, but also for its corporate character. Certainly Christian worship is corporate, like the worship of Israel and that of other religions both ancient and modern. But is there a difference in the corporateness of the Christian Church which sets it apart from other worshipping communities? And if so, what is it?

It is not difficult to see the distinction when we compare the worship of the Church with that of Hinduism, the religion with which the writer, as a missionary in India, has lived in frequent contact. The contrast between Christianity and Hinduism is wider, to be sure, than that of differences in worship. The authors of *The Cambridge Shorter History of India* preface their work with an account of the difficulties which face the historian of ancient India, because there has been no writing of Indian history—not even chronicles—until recent times. Dates have to be conjectured from references in the literature of other nations (e.g. Greece and China) and deductions made concerning the life of the people in a given period from the non-historical writings of that period. This need cause no surprise in a country where, for the adherents of the classical doctrine[1] of the dominant religion, history has no ultimate meaning and life itself is in the last resort an illusion. Nor would a history of Hindu worship, which might be more easily compiled than a social and political history, seeing that most of India's ancient literature is religious in character, be of any vital interest to Hindus of the present day. The many rites and ceremonies of Hinduism are only manifestations of the illusory variety of life: underlying them all is the undifferentiated and impersonal unity of *Brahman-atman*, the soul of the universe. Worship, in such a view, is offered by the individual who is himself only a temporary and illusory embodiment of the world-soul. There is an element of corporateness; but it is only due to the fact that the individual must fulfil the *dharma* or moral and religious law of the community to which he belongs, and worship according to its customary rites.

Islam may seem at first sight to have a greater sense of corporateness; but is the Muslim, even when he prostrates himself in a large assembly at a mosque, doing any more than repeating his private prayers in public, prayers which he could equally well utter alone? It is not surprising that, when Allah, with his inscrutable and arbitrary will, is conceived as 'caring not' whether men are saved or damned, there should be little in Islam corresponding to the biblical 'Church'.

When we turn to the Bible, we are in a different world. First of all there is the faith of Israel in the living God, the Lord of history. History has meaning as the scene of God's action, and the history of worship is the history of God's ordinances for his chosen people. That worship is bound to be corporate, because it is the worship of the people of God.

1 Resurgent Hinduism has, of course, given a new meaning to history in modern India.

Moreover, at the centre of the Passover and other great festivals is the remembrance of the historical events which constituted the call of Israel and its birth as a nation; and running through all the nation's literature is the hope that the Day of the Lord will come and the destiny of Israel as God's people will be fulfilled. This remembrance of the past and expectation for the future give to Israel's worship a unity running throughout.

But the corporateness of Israel's worship is limited by the wall of partition which divides Jew from Gentile. Its privileges are confined to those of a single race. The fullness of corporate worship could only be realized when it became possible to write, 'In Christ there is neither Jew nor Gentile . . .'

The corporateness, therefore, of Christian worship transcends the human boundaries of class and race; but more than that, it is also an expression of the inmost nature of the worshipping Church. For students of the New Testament the Greek word *koinonia*—'fellowship' or 'sharing in'—is quite fundamental to their understanding of the meaning both of the Church and of the meeting together of the Church. Again, when St. Paul says of the Lord's Supper, 'Any one who eats and drinks without discerning the body eats and drinks judgement upon himself' (1 Corinthians 11. 29), he is uttering his final word of reproof to those who had separated themselves into factions even when they assembled as the Church for worship. To partake of the Body of Christ in the Sacrament is to acknowledge membership of his Body the Church, for the two are identical. (See also 1 Cor. 10. 16, 17). Failure in the fellowship of the Body, the Church, is the same as failure to discern the sacramental Body and draws down divine judgement.

When Paul wrote these words, the majority of those who claimed membership of the Body of Christ were still alive and expected to be united with their Lord at his coming again without passing through the experience of death. Yet in the following verse (11. 30) he admits that 'some have died' or 'fallen asleep'. But the implication is that they have by no means ceased to be members of the Body of Christ. They too are part of the Church expectant of whom the living members 'proclaim the Lord's death until he comes' (5. 26) every time they celebrate the Eucharist. Every Eucharist, therefore—and indeed every gathering together of two or three in Christ's name—is one with the worship of the Church in every age from the Resurrection to the Parousia (Christ's coming again). This is the justification for our studying the worship of the Church in the past as well as the present, as we are about to do. It is no mere antiquarian research, but an attempt to realize our unity with our brethren who have 'fallen asleep' from St. Paul's time to the present day and who await with us the final resurrection. Our unity with them and the unity of the Church's worship, is, therefore, 'eschatological', i.e. related to the End in which God's purpose will be completed. This is why in the Eucharist we join our praise with that of 'angels and archangels and the whole company of heaven'. The fellowship of Christian worship is not based upon the passing unities of race or community, but upon God's purpose to 'sum up all things in Christ'. It is the fellowship of humanity redeemed in Christ and awaiting the fulfilment of that redemption, and therefore constantly submitted to the judgement and renewal of divine revelation in the present. This is why we end our prayers 'through Jesus Christ our Lord'. As C. H. Dodd has written in his essay 'The Prologue to the Fourth Gospel and Christian Worship'[1] :

If, then, our worship is truly conditioned by the revelation of God in Christ the Word, it cannot avoid this ordained pattern of judgment and renewal. Christian worship does not begin with a surge of joyous or exalted feeling which carries a man out of himself into regions of spiritual bliss. It begins when in the presence of Christ crucified we are placed under the judgment of God. 'Now is the judgment of this world', is the declaration which John has placed

[1] *Studies in the Fourth Gospel* (ed. F. L. Cross, London, 1957).

over the scene of the crucifixion. It stands over every
anamnesis (memorial) of the death of Christ. And judgment must begin from the house of God (as we read in
1 Peter 4. 17, echoing the prophets). As we make our
humble confession of sin, the judgment has begun, and as
we proceed, the historical pattern fulfils itself afresh in us,
for judgment is followed by renewal : the life of God is
imparted to us through Christ risen from the dead. The
way in which this pattern is worked out in traditional forms
of liturgy I need not illustrate.

Let the reader find his own illustrations in the chapters
which follow.

CHAPTER 2

THE LEGACY OF ISRAEL

THE LIKENESS OF JEWISH AND CHRISTIAN
WORSHIP

WE have already noted in the previous chapter that the
worship of Israel stands beside Christian worship in contrast
to the worship of other religions. First of all there is the
common basis of both in the action of God in history.
Secondly the corporateness of Israelite and Christian worship
is more emphatic—perhaps we should say dogmatic—and
fundamental to its nature than is the case with the worship of
other faiths. We must now pass on to consider in greater
detail the connexion between the two which arises from the
fact that historically the Church which is 'the new Israel' came
to birth as a movement within the old Israel.

The early chapters of Acts make it clear that the first
believers were orthodox Jews who continued for some time
after Pentecost to worship with their fellow-countrymen in the
Temple and the synagogues. And, even after the Church had
broken the bounds of Judaism, it was evidently still from the
synagogues that the earliest missionaries won many of their
converts, whether these were Jews and proselytes, or Gentile
'God-fearers' who had been attracted by Judaism without
becoming full adherents. Of such, no doubt, were the house-
hold of Stephanas whom Paul exhorts the Church of Corinth
to obey[1] and the leaders in the Church of Thessalonica whom
he addresses in 1 Thessalonians 5. 14-22.[2] It was natural that

[1] 1 Cor. 16. 15f. cf. Acts 18. 4-8.

[2] cf. Acts 17. 4.

under such leadership the Church should take over from the synagogue much of its tradition of worship including its ordered reading of Scripture. This *direct* contribution of the worship of Judaism to the worship of the Church will be considered in the latter part of this chapter.

THE CHURCH'S WORSHIP AND THE OLD TESTAMENT

But, prior to this, there was, and still is, an impact of the faith of Israel on the worship of the Church which is *indirect* rather than direct, theological rather than liturgical. The Church owes to Israel a worship based on the knowledge of God as Lord, not only of nature but of history. Israel's worship begins in the natural seasons of the year—spring and autumn, seed-time and harvest—but always moves on to the historical, or rather to a theological interpretation of history by the prophets as revealing the character and purpose of God.

The supreme example of this is the Passover, the primitive spring festival of the shepherd, intended to promote fertility among his flocks and to ward off evil from himself and them. In Exodus, however, it has become the commemoration of Israel's escape from Egypt as a divine act of redemption. And the same principle of reinterpretation is to be seen at work throughout the cultic[1] year. In offering, for instance, the first fruits of his harvest, the worshipper is bidden to say, 'A wandering Aramaean was my father, and he went down into Egypt and sojourned there, few in number . . . and the LORD brought us out of Egypt with a mighty hand and an outstretched arm, with great terror, with signs and wonders, and he brought us into this place and gave us this land, a land flowing with milk and honey. And behold, now I bring the first of the fruit of ·the ground, which thou, O LORD, hast given me.'[2]

[1] cult = system of worship.
[2] Deut. 26. 1-11.

In other words, worship for the Israelite is essentially a remembrance or memorial of God's saving action. It is important that we should understand the meaning of this. By 'remembrance' the Hebrew never meant merely mental activity as is connoted by the word in modern speech. It was always something concrete—i.e. visible or audible—which embodied and demonstrated in the present the act 'remembered' from the past. This might be the case not only with ritual and ceremonial, but with the actions of common life as well. The Israelite must give rest to his slaves on the Sabbath[1] and treat them justly and charitably on other occasions[2] as a concrete 'remembrance' of what God had done for him or his forefathers as slaves in Egypt. Such charity is, therefore, an act of worship, and worship is related to life. There is a direct line of development between the Old Testament presentation of ethics as part of worship and the oft-repeated insistence in the Epistles that the believer's conduct must be motivated by the fact of his salvation through Christ and be a living expression of that salvation.[3]

This links up with a feature of Israel's worship to which much attention has been paid by recent scholars. How, they have asked, did the ordinary Israelite know these acts of God which were to govern his daily life? How was what we have in the Old Testament—law, history, prophecy, and psalmody—composed and handed down from generation to generation? Their conclusion is that it was not generally written down in the first place but transmitted orally, at any rate in the pre-exilic period. It is also clear that the narrator of Israel's history, the prophet who interpreted that history and applied it to the situation of his own time and the psalmist who sang of the glorious acts of the Lord, were all connected with Israel's cultic centres, the local shrines or the Temple at Jerusalem. Their utterance were as much part of Israel's

1 Deut. 5. 14, 15.
2 Deut. 15. 15; 16. 12; 24. 18, 22.
3 Col. 2. 20 - 4. 1, 1 Pet. 2. 18-25, Eph. 4-6.

worship as sermons and hymns are of Christian worship. Their remembrance of God's acts in worship was intended to lead to Israel's remembrance of them in life. There was, therefore, in Israel's worship a ministry of the Word as well as a ministry of sacrifice, and the Church has inherited this in its ministry of the Word which stands beside the ministry of the sacraments.

All these insights of Israel's worship find their fulfilment in the worship of the Church. Just as in Israel's calendar the natural seasons became the memorial of God's revelation in history, so too in the Church's calendar they have become the means of unfolding step by step from Advent to Pentecost the meaning of God's self-revelation in Christ. Nature's time is sanctified to become the time of revelation. And, just as the supreme instance under the old covenant was the Passover, so also for the Christian it is 'Christ our Passover Lamb, sacrificed for us', who is brought to living 'remembrance' in the present. This happens not only on Good Friday and Easter, the greater Passover of a greater redemption; it is also the meaning of every Eucharist and, indeed, of every Lord's Day, which, as the first day of the week, is a 'memorial' or corporate expression and embodiment in worship of the resurrection.

THE CHURCH'S WORSHIP AND THAT OF THE SYNAGOGUE

So far we have been considering the inspiration derived in Christian worship from the Old Testament, a factor which has been creative and formative from the beginnings of the Church until now. It remains for us to consider the more direct and historical influence of the Judaism of the first century which was the religious setting in which the early Church came into being.

The earliest Christians, all of them Jews, doubtless regarded themselves and were regarded by their fellow-countrymen as a sect within the old Israel. Although their Leader had been put to death at the instigation of the Sanhedrin and they themselves were regarded with suspicion from the first by the same governing body of the Jewish nation and were subject to sporadic outbursts of persecution, this did not prevent their worshipping in the temple and the synagogues.

Worship in the temple was only possible for the Church in Jerusalem and, in any case, ceased with its destruction in A.D. 70, if not long before that. There was, therefore, little or no direct influence on Christian worship from this source; though Jewish sacrificial ideas have at all times played their part in the development of eucharistic doctrine, and the Psalms which were the hymns of the temple came into Christian worship through the worship of the synagogue where they were chanted antiphonally.

For the Jew, whether of Palestine or of the dispersion, the synagogue was the normal place of public worship, and we have already noted how Paul and presumably other mission-aries of the New Testament era began their work by preaching in it wherever they went and gained from it converts who were to be the leaders of the newly-founded Churches and who, when they withdrew from the synagogue, carried away with them a large measure of its heritage of worship.

Though lectionaries were a later development in Judaism, it has been established that fixed lessons from the Law and lessons chosen by the leader from the Prophets had already become a regular part of Jewish worship by the beginning of the Christian era.[1] Although the only reference in the New Testament to the reading of Scripture in public worship is to be found in 1 Timothy 4. 13, knowledge of the Scriptures is assumed by the writers of the Epistles and in other early Christian writings, e.g., 1 Clement which was written at the

---

[1] W. O. E. Oesterley, *The Jewish Background of the Christian Liturgy* (pp. 38ff). I am indebted to this book for several points in this section. See also our Lord's choice of a lesson from the Prophets, Luke 4. 16-20.

end of the first century. This can hardly have developed in the Church without public reading; for at that time private possession of copies of the Scriptures was rare. Further, in Colossians 4. 16 we see the beginning of the reading of specifically Christian writings in the public assemblies of the Church, though these were not regarded as Scripture at this time.

Besides this direct injunction by St. Paul to read his epistles in Church, there is evidence that other parts of the New Testament were compiled with public worship in view. For instance, G. D. Kilpatrick[1] concludes that Matthew 'was compiled out of materials which had already been read and expounded in the services of the Church and that the evangelist composed it to serve this purpose more fully in the future'. This suggests that Mark and other sources used by Matthew had already been used for liturgical reading before the latter was compiled. The liturgical character of such passages in the Gospels as the account of the last Supper and the narratives of the Passion is widely recognized. Again, the teaching concerning Christian conduct and worship, found in the Pauline and other Epistles, appears to have been drawn in large measure from a common tradition of public instruction of catechumens. It was only a short step to introduce the repetition of this instruction, as we have it in the New Testament, into the meetings of worship of those already baptized.

Justin Martyr[2] is the first Christian writer to refer to the reading of Scripture as an established part of worship. He says, 'The assembly takes place and the memoirs of the Apostles' (by which he presumably means the Gospels) 'or the writings of the prophets are read as far as time permits. Then, when the reader has finished, the president preaches in admonition and exhortation to imitate these excellent utterances.' This indicates that a sermon, which was also part of the

---

[1] *The Origins of the Gospel according to St. Matthew,* p. 100.
[2] *Apology,* 1. 67.

synagogue worship, followed the readings. So far, as in the synagogue of the time, there was no lectionary, but the choice of the passages and their length were evidently left to the reader or the president. The late development of the lectionary in no way lessens its value as a means of declaring 'the whole counsel of God' to the Church by means of a planned series of lections, instead of leaving the choice to the more limited preferences of the minister.

Besides the scriptural lections, the general form and spirit of the prayers which have come down to us from the early Church show marked traces of the influence of the synagogue. Even the hours of prayer mentioned in Acts as observed by the Church—the third (i.e. 9.0 a.m.), the sixth and the ninth[1] —which were still customary in the time of Tertullian, were the daily hours of prayer in the synagogue, where they may have been fixed by the hours of sacrifice in the temple. And, just as the Shemoneh Esreh,[1] or Eighteen Benedictions, which formed the central core of the worship of the synagogue were said in whole or in part at each of these three services, so too the *Didache*, or 'Teaching of the Twelve Apostles', mentions that Christians are to say the Lord's Prayer three times daily. There is evidence that the prayer itself has affinities with prayers used in the synagogue and that in the Matthean version it has been amplified by the addition of phrases from Jewish prayers. Origen, Cyprian and Tertullian also mention two other hours of prayer which had come into practice in the Church later, at cock-crow (the beginning of the fourth watch of the night, 3.0 a.m.) and before retiring to rest. Thus we see the Church borrowing from the synagogue a rule of prayer which was later to develop into the Services of the Hours.

1 Acts 2. 15, 10. 9, 3. 1.

2 The *Shemoneh Esreh,* particularly such benedictions as 'Blessed be God who raiseth the dead', may well have been the pattern of the statements and benedictions of a credal character which are found frequently in the New Testament and from which the later baptismal creeds may be said to have developed. See J. N. D. Kelly, *Early Christian Creeds* (London, Longmans, 1950), ch. 1.

With regard to individual prayers, Dr. W. O. E. Oesterley[1] has shown that many of the prayers in such works as 1 Clement, the *Prayer-book of Sarapion* and the *Didache* are adaptations of synagogue prayers. One important instance in other liturgies is the *Sanctus* ('Holy, Holy, Holy') which became a universal element in eucharistic worship. Besides its origin in Isaiah 6. 3, this may have been inspired by the *Kedushah* or 'Sanctification' (of the name of God) which occurs in three places in the synagogue order of worship, though direct derivation from the latter is uncertain.[2]

Doubtless the most widespread instance of Jewish influence in Christian worship is the *Amen* which occurs at the end of Christian, as of Jewish, prayers. The significance of this is that all in the congregation by saying it associate themselves with the person praying, thus making the act of prayer corporate. St. Paul clearly attached importance to this liturgical word.[3] So too, Justin Martyr in the second century, writing of the Eucharist, says, 'The President offers up prayers and thanksgiving according to his ability, and the people cry aloud saying, *Amen.*' Indeed the references to the *Amen* in early Christian writings are too numerous to quote.

The origins of the Eucharist will be considered further in a later chapter. It may, however, be said here, that in addition to the debt owed to the synagogue in the prayers and lections of the first part of the liturgy, the shape which the Eucharist liturgy took seems, in large measure, to have been governed by its connexion with the ritual of Jewish meals. When the New Israel transcended the Old and became separated from its parent, it did not leave empty handed, but carried away a great heritage from the worship of the latter which was to be formative in its own worship.

[1] Op. cit., pp. 125-147.

[2] For the evidence see J. A. Jungmann, *Missarum Sollemnia* (Benziger, 1955), (Eng. tr. *The Mass of the Roman Rite*), vol. ii, pp. 132f. nn.

[3] 1 Cor. 14. 16, 2 Cor. 1. 20.

CHAPTER 3

CHRISTIAN INITIATION

BAPTISM IN THE NEW TESTAMENT

FROM the beginning of the Church's history to be a Christian was never a matter of inward conviction only or of mere enrolment. The command of Peter, as recorded in Acts 2. 38, to those who heard the first apostolic preaching was, 'Repent, and be baptized every one of you in the name of Jesus Christ for the forgiveness of your sins; and you shall receive the gift of the Holy Spirit.' Entrance into the Church has been, therefore, from apostolic times[1] effected by means of a sacramental act. This consisted invariably of the use of water which came to be accompanied at an early period by the laying on of hands and anointing with oil. The relation of these latter actions to Baptism with water will have to be considered during the course of this chapter. Suffice it to say at this point that this rite of initiation was believed to confer both forgiveness of sins and the gift of the Holy Spirit.

It is clear that Baptism underwent development within the New Testament period itself. At first it was given 'in the name of the Lord Jesus' (Acts 8. 16, 19. 5). The formula 'in the name of the Father, and of the Son, and of the Holy Spirit' (Matt. 28. 19) soon came to be used universally; but was, in all probability, not current in the earliest days. Again, are we to regard the laying on of hands by the Apostles (Acts 8. 17 and 19. 6) as the normal accompaniment of Baptism

---

[1] There are of course Jewish antecedents to Baptism, and Christian Baptism owed an immediate debt to John the Baptist: it is still too early to come to a conclusion from the study of the Dead Sea scrolls whether his baptism had any connexion with the conjectured practice of the Qumran sect.

with water at this time, or did Luke record these actions as exceptional? Many scholars incline to the latter view. If so, the widespread acceptance of this practice was a later development.

The references in Acts to an at least occasional practice of the laying on of hands are explicit and clear : not so with the evidence in the New Testament for the use of *chrism* (anointing with oil). The 'anointing' mentioned in 1 John 20. 20, 27 as received by believers may be this liturgical action; but the emphasis in the passage is on the spiritual enlighten- ment which is conferred by the anointing, and the word more probably signifies an inward experience—the anointing of the Spirit—rather than an outward ceremony.   Again, Paul's words, 'He has put his seal upon us and given us his Spirit in our hearts as a guarantee' in 2 Cor. 1. 22 (cf. Eph. 1. 13, 4. 30) have been claimed as evidence for the theory that the Apostle knew of a ritual action combined with Baptism by water which he regarded as 'the seal' of Baptism in that it signified the conferring of the Spirit. Additional support for this view has been looked for in Paul's typological interpretation of the ancient Israelites' 'baptism' in the cloud (= the Spirit) and in the sea (= water) as prefiguring Christian Baptism (1 Cor. 10. 2ff.). Here again, however, it seems preferable to take 'the seal' as referring to the inward action of God and the experi- ence of the believer by which he is marked as belonging to Christ rather than as denoting any outward rite.[1]

Hebrews 6. 2 associates 'baptisms' with the laying on of hands and may reflect a regular joining together of the two actions in the Church in which it was written; but it is uncertain whether the Greek word *baptismōn* should be trans- lated 'baptisms' or 'ablutions'. The only indisputably universal sacrament of initiation in the Gospels and the apostolic Church is Baptism with water. This itself, it seems, was regarded as the effective sign, not only of the washing away of sin, but also of the gift of the Spirit. And yet the two

[1] See G. W. H. Lampe, *The Seal of the Spirit.*

remain, in a sense, distinct from each other, and the outward rite is only preparatory to, and needs to be sealed by, the inward gift.

INITIATION IN THE AGE OF THE FATHERS

The argument that Baptism with water even in the apostolic period needed to be completed by other ritual actions, concerning which we have expressed doubt, is an attempt to discover in the New Testament the beginnings of the developed practice of Christian initiation for which there is ample evidence in the two centuries following; though, even in this period, we cannot find anything like uniformity. The *Didache* has no reference either to chrism or laying on of hands in its detailed instructions for Baptism, though admittedly, in view of the uncertain date and place of origin of this work, the value of its evidence is difficult to assess. More important is the testimony of Justin Martyr who in his *First Apology* describes Baptism as it was practised in the Roman Church soon after the middle of the second century. The candidates had to undergo a period of preparation and instruction and make profession of their faith and promise to live according to the teaching they received, after which they were baptized. After the baptism had been administered, the candidate was brought to the assembled congregation by those who had assisted at the rite 'to make public prayers for ourselves, for him who has been illuminated and for all men everywhere'. These prayers belonged evidently to the preliminary part of the order of the Eucharist which then proceeded to its completion in Communion and at which the newly baptized would receive his first Communion. Justin says, 'This washing is called illumination' and, in the same passage, he speaks of it as 'the way of regeneration'; but he makes no mention of the laying on of hands or the chrism.

In the third century the more elaborate pattern of initiation which is typical of the period of the Fathers becomes manifest, Tertullian, for instance, writes : 'The flesh is washed that the soul may be rid of its stain; the flesh is anointed that the soul may be sanctified; the flesh is covered by the laying on of the hand that the soul may be illuminated by the Spirit; the flesh is fed with the Body and Blood of Christ that the soul too may be nourished from God.'[1]

We see in this passage a brief summary of the sequence of the rite as then widely administered : immersion in water, chrism (consignation, or signing with the cross doubtless came in at this point), laying on of hands, Holy Communion. The gift of the Spirit is especially attributed to the laying on of hands; indeed, in another passage, Tertullian denies that the Spirit is given through Baptism in water.

In *The Apostolic Tradition* of Hippolytus a detailed account of Baptism is given, probably as practised in Rome in the second century. From this we learn that the candidates went naked into the water and were immersed three times, three separate questions being asked, one before each immersion, concerning their belief in the Father, the Son and the Holy Spirit.[2]

After emerging from the water, the candidates dressed and were presented to the Bishop who first laid his hands on them and then anointed them with oil saying the words, 'I anoint thee with the holy oil in God the Father Almighty and in Jesus Christ and in the Holy Spirit.' It seems clear that in this form of Baptism the gift of the Spirit was particularly associated with the chrism, and it is to be noted that the name of the Trinity was used at this point and not at the immersion in water. As with Tertullian, Baptism immediately preceded the Eucharist at which the newly baptized received their first Communion. It remains for us to note a significant variation from the general order as found in these two writers and

---

[1] *Concerning the Resurrection of the Flesh*, 8.

[2] The present Roman rite still retains the interrogatory baptismal Creed in immediate proximity to the administration of Baptism and modern baptismal rites have been criticized by liturgists for obscuring this ancient order by the interposition of baptismal prayers.

elsewhere. In the Churches of Syria it was the custom to give the chrism *before* immersion in the water instead of afterwards. The Syrian Churches of today, including those of Malabar, have an anointing with oil both before and after the affusion of water.[1]

This great rite was preceded by a long catechumenate, often lasting for three years. Baptism was normally given on the early morning of Easter Day (with an additional baptismal festival at Pentecost for those who had not been presented at Easter) and before this the catechumens received about three weeks or more intensive instruction accompanied by fasting, scrutiny of their way of life, exorcism by means of 'exsufflation' (breathing in the candidate's face), the renunciation of the Devil, the teaching of the Creed and its recitation by the candidates and other symbolic actions. Hippolytus also mentions that at the Easter Eucharist, at which the newly baptized received their first Communion, they are given between the reception of the Bread and the Cup two other cups, one filled with milk and honey and the other with water. This is interpreted symbolically by Hippolytus as the sign of their entrance into the Promised Land. Jungmann, incidentally, regards this as 'harking back to a time when the meal was interposed before the consecration of the chalice'.[2]

Other symbolic actions—the putting on of white robes and the holding of lighted tapers—though not recorded by Hippolytus, also belong to an early date. They are still retained in the classical rites and have been reintroduced as optional ceremonies in some revisions of Reformation baptismal services, e.g., those of the Church of India, Pakistan, Burma and Ceylon and the Church of South India.

The whole rite is impressive in its continuity from catechumenate to Communion. The Church's pre-baptismal

[1] For a full description of the rite as practised in the Syrian Churches of Kerala today see L. W. Brown, *The Indian Christians of St. Thomas*, pp. 250-254.

[2] *Missarum Sollemnia*, Eng. tr., I. p. 15. See also the next chapter.

teaching—the ministry of the Word—and her administration of the two Sacraments of the Gospel to those deemed fitted by faith and hope to enter her fellowship form one undivided whole. There has, however, been a great elaboration of supplementary ceremonies since the apostolic age. Though the elaboration was a departure from apostolic simplicity, the increased length of the catechumenate and the greater thoroughness of instruction was a necessary development. In New Testament times the urgency of the expectation of the end of the age had led the early evangelists to baptize with only a minimum of preparation. Now the very length and complexity of Christian initiation helped to stress its overriding importance in the life of the Church, as did also the fact that it was presided over by the Bishop as chief pastor of the Church. It was the Bishop who administered the laying on of hands and the chrism, though he was assisted by presbyters and deacons at the immersion in water.

The distinction between Baptism with water and Baptism with the Spirit has, as we have seen, its basis in the New Testament. There is, however, in the second and third century developments which we have been studying a certain falling away from the primitive insight in this matter. Though there is evidence in Acts of an incipient tendency to associate the gift of the Spirit with the laying on of hands by the Apostles, for the New Testament as a whole the gift of the Spirit is a transcendent and eschatological reality of which the sacrament is a sign. For Paul it is the earnest or guarantee of our inheritance, the first foretaste of the Age to come,[1] and in the Fourth Gospel it is birth from above, the act of the Spirit who blows where he wills.[2] In the post-apostolic development, on the other hand, we see a movement to confine and canalize the working of the Spirit in sacramental channels. Neither Justin's simple identification of the washing in water with spiritual enlightenment nor the notion of Tertullian and Hippolytus that the Spirit was conferred by the chrism or the laying on of

[1] Eph. 1. 14.   [2] John 3. 3, 8.

C

hands, nor its association a little later, particularly in the West, with the signing with the cross, are in accord with the New Testament. The gift of the Spirit is a God-given experience and cannot be limited by a liturgical act. It is doubtless well that there was a chronic uncertainty among the Fathers as to which of these many liturgical acts they should regard as conferring the Spirit.

This great sequence of early Christian initiation arose in a missionary Church whose life was set in a predominantly pagan environment. It is only appropriate to believer's Baptism which is assumed to be the norm. Many have advocated a return to it in a modified form in the younger Churches of our day, where the position of the Christian community is similar to that of the early Church. In these younger Churches there has been a revival of the catechumenate, which lapsed with the spread of infant Baptism. In some dioceses of the Anglican Communion the early continuity of Confirmation and first Communion with Baptism has been restored in the case of candidates able to answer for themselves; but in most areas the custom has been prevalent of separating Confirmation from Baptism by a period of about a year so as to give time for further instruction. This practice has been widely defended on the ground that new converts ought to be baptized as soon as possible, as a lengthy period of preparation is apt to strain their patience and damp their enthusiasm; whereas those to be admitted to communicant status should have reached a greater degree of maturity in faith and life.[1]

BAPTISM AND CONFIRMATION—
THE MIDDLE AGES

To return to the early centuries, the practice which we have outlined above did not continue unchanged for long. As

[1] See an interesting analysis of this subject by M. A. C. Warren in *Baptism and Confirmation* (Church Book Room Press). I am indebted for several points in this chapter to an essay in the same book by F. J. Taylor.

the Church grew in numbers and moved out of the period
when the majority of its members were converts from pagan-
ism, the catechumenate declined. Infant Baptism, which may
have been practised from New Testament times, but was still
the exception in the time of Tertullian and disapproved by
him, became the norm. Bishops became preoccupied with
civil as well as ecclesiastical affairs and, in any case, found it a
physical impossibility to be present at every Baptism to
administer the chrism and laying on of hands. In this situation there were two alternatives before the Church : either to
separate Baptism from the other ceremonies, or to allow
presbyters to administer the whole rite without the presence
of the Bishop. The course of Church History reveals that the
East and the West differed in their choice, the West following
the former practice and the East the latter.

This general statement requires further definition. To take
the practice of the Eastern Churches first, the connexion of
the rite with the Bishop has not been entirely severed. The
oil used in administering the chrism is consecrated either by
the Metropolitan or by the diocesan Bishop, and he is still
regarded as the celebrant of the rite of which the presbyters
are only the administrants. The practice of the laying on of
hands has lapsed; but the giving of the chrism is regarded by
modern Orthodox theologians as an indispensable element in
Baptism. The whole rite is administered to infants who afterwards receive Communion and are regarded as full communicant members of the Church. This tradition, while it preserves
the continuity of the ancient rite of initiation, leaves un-
answered the question as to how an infant may become a
participant in what is essentially an adult experience.

In the West, while it was impossible for the Bishop to be
present at every Baptism, the Bishops were not willing to give
up their part in the rite of initiation. They continued to insist
that the chrism and the imposition of hands was their pre-
rogative, not without protest from a section of the presbyters,
of whom Jerome was the most notable protagonist. This

necessitated the division of the rite of initiation into two parts, the first, Baptism with water to be given normally in infancy, the second, which came in the Middle Ages to be called Confirmation (i.e., 'strengthening'), was administered by the Bishop a few years later. Confirmation during the Middle Ages had a varied history. The present practice of the Roman Catholic Church, which represents what was finally established, is for children to be confirmed at the age of seven, usually *after* receiving their first Communion. The Bishop makes the sign of the cross with the holy oil or chrism on the forehead of each.[1] The imposition of hands which precedes the signing with the oil has ceased to be performed individually and is represented in the rite only by the Bishop's stretching his hands over the whole company of the candidates. Further, the protest of Jerome and others against exclusively episcopal Confirmation has not been without its effect in the history of the Western Church. Roman priests are permitted to perform the rite in certain circumstances, particularly in remote places where the services of a bishop are unobtainable.

Together with these changes in the form of the rite in the West went a significant development in the theological meaning attributed to it. Baptism with water was regarded as conferring regeneration and the gift of the Spirit. It was a rite complete in itself. Although, as we have seen, the evidence of the New Testament is not entirely clear at this point, the Church may be said to have thus returned in a measure to the apostolic standpoint. There was however the important difference that infant Baptism had now become the norm, and the vital question of the relation of regeneration and the gift of the Spirit to conversion experience cannot be said to have been faced. Confirmation, which was still given to young

[1] After the signing with the oil the Bishop strikes each candidate lightly on the cheek and says 'Peace be with thee'. This may be a survival of the kiss of peace with which the Bishop in the time of Hippolytus concluded the rite of initiation. The Church of South India has revived this by giving the greeting of peace in its Syrian form to the newly confirmed.

children incapable of mature faith, was regarded as 'strengthening' a gift already given. It was not surprising if some asked whether it was necessary at all. The medieval uncertainty concerning both the form and the intention of Confirmation prepared the way for its rejection by many of the Churches of the Reformation.

BAPTISM AND CONFIRMATION—
THE REFORMATION

Article XXV of the Anglican Articles of Religion numbers Confirmation among 'those five commonly called Sacraments' which 'are not to be counted for Sacraments of the Gospel', as are Baptism and the Lord's Supper, 'for that they have not any visible sign or ceremony ordained of God'. This represents a position widely adopted by the Reformers. Confirmation is, according to it, to be treated as an ecclesiastical ordinance rather than as a Sacrament.

LUTHERANS AND ANGLICANS

There has been a wide variety of practice in the Churches of the Reformation. The Lutheran Churches and the Anglican Communion stand closest together, as might be expected from the fact that Cranmer was in close consultation with Lutherans in Europe at the time of the drafting of the first English Book of Common Prayer. How much Cranmer owed to the Germans is a point upon which Lutherans and Anglicans are not likely to agree !

The Lutheran and Anglican baptismal rites have several passages in common, notably the typological use of the Flood and the passage through the Red Sea. This is found in the Roman tradition, but the wording is new. In the first Anglican Prayer Book Cranmer retained from the Western Rite a signing with the cross on the forehead and on the breast near the beginning of the service which came before the exorcism of the devil. Lutherans, except in some Lutheran Churches of America who have omitted the signing with the cross altogether, still retain it at this point, while Anglicans since the publication of the second Prayer Book in 1552 have it after the act of Baptism accompanied by a declaration of reception into the Church. At this point in the Lutheran service there is an imposition of the minister's hand on the head of the newly baptized, whether infant or adult.

Both Churches have retained the name and rite of Confirmation, of which for Anglicans the Bishop is the sole minister, while in Lutheran Churches the local minister performs the rite, even where they have retained episcopacy. The pastoral and doctrinal intention of both orders is the same, namely, to enable those baptized in infancy who have attained years of discretion publicly to accept for themselves the promises made at their baptism, and to ask God to 'strengthen' them with the Holy Spirit whom they have received in Baptism. The medieval doctrine of Confirmation is here followed. The Lutheran Churches, however, have taken greater liberty of local variation than the Anglican. In the Church of Sweden, for instance, the minister may extend his hands towards the candidates, as in the Roman rite; but in other Churches there is a rubric prescribing that he should lay his hand or hands on the head of each candidate. Neither Anglicans nor Lutherans use the sign of the cross or the chrism in Confirmation. The United Lutheran Church in America has in addition a giving of the right hand of fellowship as a sign that the candidate is a full member of the Church. This Church does not confirm those who have received believers' Baptism.

THE REFORMED CHURCHES

To turn to other Churches of the Reformation, in the French Reformed Church the minister lays his hands on the head of each candidate for Confirmation, saying, 'I confirm thee in the union of Baptism, in the name of the Father and of the Son and of the Holy Spirit'. In the Confirmation service of the Book of Common Order of the Church of Scotland the minister either raises his hand in blessing over the candidates or lays it on the head of each. But, although Calvin commended Confirmation by the laying on of hands, many of the Reformed Churches have a service of admission to Holy Communion in which the action of laying on of hands has been discontinued as scarcely relevant in view of the fact that this service is regarded, not as the completion of Baptism, but as the individual's acceptance by faith of his incorporation into the Church by Baptism. This is, in general, except for the Baptists, of whom we must speak later, the practice of other non-episcopal Churches. Some give the right hand of fellowship to those to be admitted. This, together with the confession of faith, asserts the candidate's new status of responsible membership in the congregation. All these Churches avoid using the word 'regeneration' in connexion with Baptism, asserting with much support from the New Testament that regeneration is the act of God which creates faith in the believer and of which Baptism is only the outward and visible sign.

THE CHURCH OF SOUTH INDIA

In the Church of South India the Order for Holy Baptism has in it elements derived both from Reformed and Anglican sources, both of which have been submitted to revision in the light of Scripture and the ancient rites. There is a petition in the litany which precedes the act of Baptism that the candidates may be 'born anew into the fellowship of thy Church', and that 'in one Spirit they may be baptized into one body.' Emphasis is laid on what has been called the 'proleptic' character of Baptism, i.e., that it is a present foretaste of a future promise and that throughout our lives we are called to 'become what we are'. Confirmation is by the laying on of hands and is defined as 'being established in faith by the Holy Spirit', the assertion being that the Holy Spirit operates in a new way in the life of the believer, as compared with his less consciously perceived and accepted guidance in the life of the child; though in both cases the Spirit works within the realm of the Church. There is a second focal point in the rite when a brief address of welcome is spoken by the whole congregation. This is intended to declare that the newly confirmed are received into the full fellowship of the Church.

Such is the variety of usage in Christendom, and the deviations from each other are particularly manifest in the Protestant Churches. It is to be noted, however, that all the Churches of the Reformation which practise either Confirmation or admission to full membership of the Church, so far from underestimating its importance, regard it with great seriousness as an important moment in the spiritual life of the candidate and in the common life of the Church. It must be preceded by careful instruction (which constitutes a revival of the ancient catechumenate), and in the preparatory part of the service itself a profession of faith on the part of the candidates is required, which is sometimes preceded by an examination either before the service or during its course. It may be claimed that this Reformation tradition gives Confirmation its proper place in the life of the individual member of the Church, as associated with his attainment of years of discretion and his acceptance for himself of the Christian way in which he may have been brought up from childhood.

THE BAPTISTS

The one great divergence from this tradition is that of the various groups of Baptists who have rejected infant Baptism as unscriptural and only administer Baptism to those who are of age to make profession of their faith. Confirmation has been rejected by them as lacking adequate Scriptural authority and as being an unnecessary adjunct to believers' Baptism.

In many Baptist Churches a service of dedication is held for children of Christian parents, thus signifying that they are within the Christian fellowship from childhood.

IS VARIETY AN OBSTACLE TO UNITY?

These differences of doctrine and practice are both the fruit of division in the Church and serious obstacles to reunion. As such they are to be deplored. In favour of variety, however, it may be said that it points to the truth that those who are born of the Spirit are subject to the wind which blows where it wills. No uniformity of sacramental order can prescribe or control the Spirit's action in the life of the believer. It may be that a permitted measure of variety, such as that which has been accepted by the Churches which have united in the Church of South India, is the right solution.

This permissive variety can be extended to include in one united Church both infant Baptism and believers' Baptism, as is evident in the proposed schemes to inaugurate the united Churches of North India, Pakistan and Lanka; though difficulties are being encountered by the negotiating Churches, particularly the question as to whether a person baptized in infancy may, if his conscience urges him to do so, undergo Baptism again as an adult. To those who adhere to infant Baptism such permission would seem to compromise the unrepeatable character accorded to Baptism in the age-long tradition of the Church. And there are still many stricter groups of Baptists who refuse to compromise by thus uniting with Christians who practise infant Baptism.

THE ONE OPERATION OF THE SPIRIT

If we believe that the operation of the Spirit is one and undivided in all sacramental acts and that Baptism is always 'proleptic', i.e. given in the present and progressively realized in the future, whether it be administered to infants or to adults who are only beginners in the Christian life, we may perhaps think that Baptism in infancy and Confirmation in adolescence is not very different in intention and in signification of the working of the Spirit within the fellowship of the Church from dedication in infancy and Baptism at an age when faith is realized; not so different, at any rate, as to be a just cause for continued division in the Church. The critical ages of human life, infancy and adolescence, both demand a sacramental act of initiation to declare effectively the grace of God which must incorporate the growing child in the Church and operate in his life if he is to 'apprehend even as he has also been apprehended'. In either way of initiation there is a solemn act of dedication and assertion of membership of the Church at both these crucial stages of human growth; and God, we may believe, blesses both ways 'with undistinguishing regard'. The affirmations, however, of those who adhere to either point of view are strongly held and not readily reconciled, and it may be that many will regard the way of approach outlined above as offering too easy a solution.

CHAPTER 4

THE EARLY HISTORY OF THE EUCHARIST

THE EUCHARIST IN THE NEW TESTAMENT

THERE was no need for the writers of the books of the New Testament to explain to their original readers what the Eucharist was and how it should be celebrated. They presume that they already know and presuppose the rite as an already established and oft repeated act of the Church's worship. This creates difficulties for us who would like to know more about the way they performed it; but it also assures us that its centrality in the Church's worship goes right back to the beginning. It was not a later development, for it underlies every stratum of the New Testament tradition.

One reason why the accounts of the Last Supper which we have in the Synoptic Gospels and 1 Corinthians 11 tell us so little detail about this event is that they have already been given a liturgical form before their inclusion in these written books. The language is liturgical in character, as can be seen most easily in the Pauline account, when we compare its style with that of the passages of St. Paul's own writing which immediately precede and follow it. He is clearly quoting a traditional narrative already used in the worship of the Church and therefore reduced to a minimum of detail required to make plain its connexion with and meaning in the rite. So too with the narratives of the Last Supper in the first three Gospels.

Not only is this true of passages in the New Testament

directly related to the Eucharist, but the liturgical character
of many other passages can be demonstrated. There is no
explicit mention, for instance, of the Eucharist in the Epistle
to the Hebrews; and yet the whole exposition of salvation
through Christ in terms of worship seems to demand a knowledge of the Eucharist, as also it has been used by the Church
throughout the ages both as a basis for eucharistic theology
and for its expression in liturgy. It is in the Eucharist that we
realize our 'boldness to enter into the holy place by the blood
of Jesus'.[1] With this may be compared such passages as
'Through him we both have our access in one Spirit unto the
Father',[2] and 'Ye also, as living stones, are built up a spiritual
house, to be a holy priesthood, to offer up spiritual sacrifices,
acceptable to God through Jesus Christ'.[3] The Priesthood
which offers the Eucharist is the priesthood of the whole
people of God, sanctified by the sacrifice of him who is both
high priest and victim and has entered into the heavenly
sanctuary.

There is much to be said for the view that parts of the
New Testament were composed for liturgical reading. This is
particularly demonstrable in St. Matthew's Gospel which
appears to have given to earlier Gospel material a liturgical
style and arrangement.[4]

There are so many connexions with the sacraments in the
Fourth Gospel that it too may have been compiled for
liturgical use,[5] while John in Revelation depicts the worship of
heaven in a manner which seems to compare it to the Eucharist on earth, and there is perhaps a eucharistic pattern
running throughout the book and leading to its climax in the
marriage supper of the Lamb.

[1] Heb. 10. 19.
[2] Eph. 2. 18.
[3] 1 Pet. 2. 5.
[4] G. D. Kilpatrick, *The Origins of the Gospel according to St. Matthew* (Oxford, 1946).
[5] O. Cullmann, *Worship in the Early Church.*

We note also at the beginning and end of Revelation, as too at the beginning and end of Paul's epistles, greetings and injunctions which are liturgical in character—'*Maranatha*' (cf. 'Amen, Come Lord Jesus', Rev. 22. 20), 'The grace of the Lord Jesus Christ be with you', the kiss of peace. Do these liturgical formulae indicate the point in the service at which these epistles were intended to be read, i.e. immediately before the breaking of the bread?[1]

We may believe that *Marana tha*—'Come Lord'—was the first eucharistic prayer and that the early Christians saw in the presence of Christ in the Eucharist an answer to it which was a foretaste of his final coming.

All this is interpreting details in the New Testament in the light of what we know of eucharistic worship in the second and third centuries; but, if these conjectures are correct, there is in the New Testament at an earlier stage of its development that same dynamic combination of liturgical order and charismatic freedom which seems to have been characteristic of the fluid eucharistic rites of the pre-Nicene Church.

It is, then, in the context of a Church worshipping in and through the Eucharist that we look back at the narratives of the Last Supper. For a detailed interpretation of the meaning of our Lord's words and actions on that night the student may be referred to J. Jeremias, *The Eucharistic Words of Jesus,* as the best treatment of this subject. We are only concerned here with the place of the Last Supper in the development of Christian Worship. In the first place, we may say that the Last Supper is best understood as the last of the series of great signs which Jesus performed in the final week of his life, the others being the riding into Jerusalem, the cleansing of the Temple and the withering of the fig tree. Linked with this is the sign of the anointing by the woman with the ointment.

Secondly, let us notice the connexion of the Last Supper with other meals recorded in the New Testament. Clearly the Last Supper was neither the first nor the last meal that Jesus

[1] O. Cullmann, op. cit.

shared with his disciples. John gives no account of the Words of Institution, but attaches his eucharistic teaching to the feeding of the five thousand; and the accounts in the Synoptic Gospels of this and the parallel miracle of the feeding of the four thousand are clearly eucharistic in their language. The Last Supper, then, is the culmination of a series of meals of religious significance over which Jesus presided during his ministry. His eating and drinking with tax collectors and sinners is a declaration of the grace of God which is more fully shown forth in the Eucharist. And in view of Christ's preaching of the Kingdom by word and sign we may see in all these meals anticipations of the eschatological messianic feast.

But, as Jeremias writes in *The Eucharastic Words of Jesus,* 'this meal on Maundy Thursday is a special one among all the other messianic meals'. If Jeremias is correct in defending the tradition that this meal is the Passover,[1] then the eucharistic words of Jesus are attached to the actions in the Passover ritual of blessing, breaking and distributing the bread and giving thanks over the cup before distributing it. We do not know whether Jesus spoke these words before or during the distribution, but the latter seems most natural. He is the Paschal Lamb of the new age and by word and sign makes his disciples participants in the sacrifice which inaugurates it.

But the Last Supper would have remained only a sorrowful memory if Jesus had died, but not risen again. It was the resurrection which established its continuation in the Eucharist, and it has not only a backward reference to previous meals of fellowship, but a forward reference to the first common meals of the disciples at which the risen Lord appeared to them.[2]

---

[1] Even if it was a Jewish meal of another type, clearly paschal associations predominated at it, and there is not much difference in the interpretation we should give to it.

[2] Acts 10. 40f., 1. 4. In the latter verse the Greek word *synalizomenos* may be translated 'taking salt with', i.e. 'eating with' (Cullmann, op. cit. p. 16), cf. also Rev. 3. 20 as 'witnessing to the belief that, as in the first post-resurrection days, so now Christ condescends to be present with his own when they assemble to break bread' (A. J. B. Higgins, *The Lord's Supper in the New Testament,* p. 62).

Indeed, we may say that these meals in which the risen Lord was made known to the disciples in the breaking of the bread were as much the origin of the Eucharist as the Last Supper itself. They were the reason too why in the primitive Jerusalem Church the believers 'partook of food with heavenly joy' (*agalliasei,* Acts 2. 46).

The fact that the meal at which Christ first spoke the words 'This is my body ... This is my blood ...' was the Passover did not prevent his disciples from repeating it in remembrance of him on occasions other than this feast. It was not difficult for them to transfer the blessing and breaking of the bread and the longer eucharistic thanksgiving said by the head of the table over the cup from the Passover to the ritual of an ordinary Jewish meal which included a thanksgiving at the breaking of the bread near the beginning, and at the end, if a large number were present, a longer prayer of thanksgiving before common participation in a cup of wine—'the cup of blessing' or 'thanksgiving'. That this transference did in fact take place is made clear by the frequency of the 'breaking of bread from house to house' recorded in Acts and by the observations of Paul on the Lord's Supper at Corinth which was evidently a fellowship meal (1 Cor. 11). This is also indicated in Paul's narrative of the Last Supper which includes the words, 'In the same way also the cup after supper ...' (11. 25) which would have liturgical point if a meal still took place between the breaking of the bread and the giving of the cup.

Other evidence that the primitive Church celebrated the Eucharist at first in the context of the customary ritual of a Jewish meal are found in the eucharistic liturgies themselves :

(i) the common Jewish greeting and response :
    The Lord be with you :
    And with thy spirit.

(ii) The versicle and response which preceded the prayer of thanksgiving over the cup. (As we shall see, this prayer was the prototype of the Christian eucharistic prayer) :

> Let us give thanks unto our Lord God :
> It is meet and right so to do.

(iii) The fact that the celebrant takes the cup into his hands, as was done at the end of the prayer of thanksgiving by the head of the table at Jewish meals.

It is doubtless wrong to suppose with H. Lietzmann (in *Messe und Herrenmahl*) that there were two types of Eucharist in the early Church, one a glad fellowship meal in remembrance of the resurrection, with no connexion with the Last Supper and the Passion, such as is mentioned in the early chapters of Acts, and the other a more solemn remembrance of Christ's death inaugurated by Paul in the churches of his foundation. Even if there were differences of emphasis in different places, all Eucharists have their dual origin both in the Last Supper and the resurrection appearances. But it is also clear from what happened at Corinth that a joyous meal could be sadly abused, and we see Paul dealing with the situation : (*a*) by reminding the Church of the solemnity of this meal in view of its connexion with Christ's death and the hope of his coming again; (*b*) by admonishing them that if anyone is hungry he should eat at home. This latter injunction was doubtless the first step in the separation of the Eucharist from its accompanying *agape* (love feast), which seems to have taken place throughout the Church by the beginning of the second century. Mark's narrative of the Last Supper is regarded by Jeremias and other scholars as more primitive in its language than Paul's narrative; but in one respect it may represent a later stage in the development of the Eucharist. The words 'after supper' do not occur in it. Had this separation of the Eucharist from the *agape* already taken place in the churches known to Mark when he wrote? It is also difficult to believe that the 'gathering together to break bread'[1] at

[1] Acts 20. 7-12.

Troas on the first day of the week (presumably Saturday night, according to Jewish reckoning) with its long preparatory ministry of the Word, as in the Eucharist of later centuries, was quite an ordinary fellowship meal intended to satisfy hunger. Perhaps it too indicates a stage in the process of separation.

Little more need be said of the *agape*. It survived as a charitable dinner in many places, but was eventually suppressed on account of the same kind of abuses as those which occurred in Corinth. There was a vestige of it in the milk and honey, given between the bread and the cup to the newly baptized at their first communion in the time of Hippolytus (see page 24). There are also scattered instances in later centuries of celebrations of the Eucharist in close relation to a meal on special occasions, e.g. Maundy Thursday. Perhaps another less direct trace of it survives today in the distribution of 'blessed bread' after the Eucharist in the Eastern Churches. This goes back to the ancient offering of the eucharistic bread and wine by the people in kind and the distribution after the service of any that had not been required for the eucharistic celebrations.

One ancient form of thanksgiving prayer, which most scholars now agree belongs to the *agape* after it had been separated, rather than to Eucharist and *agape* together, is found in *The Teaching (Didache) of the Twelve Apostles,* a work probably belonging to the second century. Even if it does not belong to the Eucharist, it may well be that many early eucharistic prayers were of this type; and we find a passage from this particular prayer finding its way into a fourth-century liturgy in Egypt.[1]

Concerning the thanksgiving thus give ye thanks :

First, concerning the cup : 'We give thanks unto thee, our Father, for the holy vine of David thy servant, which thou didst make known unto us through Jesus thy servant; *to thee be the glory for ever and ever.*'

[1] Prayer Book of Sarapion, see p. 56.

D

Concerning the broken bread : 'We give thanks unto thee, our Father, for the life and knowledge, which thou didst make known unto us through Jesus thy servant; *to thee be the glory for ever.*

'As this broken bread was scattered over the mountains and being gathered together became one, so may thy Church be gathered together from the ends of the earth into thy kingdom : *for thine is the glory and the power through Jesus Christ for ever.*'

Let no one eat or drink at your thanksgiving but those who have been baptized in the name of the Lord, for it was about this that the Lord said : 'Do not give that which is holy to the dogs.'

When you have been filled, give thanks as follows :

'We give thanks to thee, holy Father, for thy holy Name, which thou hast made to dwell in our hearts, and for the knowledge, faith and immortality which thou hast made known to us through thy servant Jesus. *To thee be glory for ever.*

'Thou, Lord, ruler of the world, hast made all things for thy Name, hast given food and drink to all for their enjoyment that they might thank thee; but to us thou hast given spiritual meat and drink, and eternal life through thy servant Jesus. Before all we give thanks to thee, for thou art mighty. *To thee be glory for ever.*

'Remember, Lord, thy Church to deliver her from every evil and to complete her in thy love; and gather her together from the four winds, as a sanctified Church, into thy kingdom which thou hast prepared for her; *for thine is the power and the glory for ever and ever.*'

'Let grace come, and let this world pass away.
Hosanna to the God of David !
If any man is holy, let him come; if any man is not, let him repent.
Marana tha. Amen.'

Revivals of the *agape* in modern times as the parish break-fast following the parish communion have not been without success in promoting fellowship. The writer recalls his impression when attending one such at Clare College, Cambridge, which included the passing around of a loaf—one of those brought up in the offertory, but not consecrated, at the Eucharist—with the recitation of a passage from the *Didache* quoted above, after which each of those who had received communion in chapel and now shared in the fellowship meal took a piece. In the Tamil area of India the feasts which are a feature of Christian festivals in many village congregations are often called 'love feasts'. Though they have their historical connexions with similar ones held by non-Christian villagers, they may nevertheless be regarded as modern instances of the *agape,* linked in thought with the eucharistic feast and reminding those who participate that, when they meet at the Lord's Table, they meet, not as individuals, but as a family.

To return to the Eucharist at the point of its separation from the *agape:* what actually happened, and how did the early Church effect this separation? We can only conjecture; but we have a pointer in the fundamental structure which is common to all the ancient liturgies and which must therefore go back to the earliest period before they developed their different characteristics. It is what Dix in *The Shape of the Liturgy* calls 'the four action shape'. The point is that this is not the 'shape' presupposed by the narratives of the Last Supper in the New Testament. There we have a seven action shape: (1) Jesus takes bread, (2) he blesses it,[1] (3) he breaks it, (4) he gives it to the disciples, (5) he takes the cup, (6) he gives thanks over it, (7) he gives it to the disciples. Presumably at the time that Paul wrote 1 Corinthians the Church still celebrated the Eucharist during a meal with this sevenfold action.

[1] or gives thanks over it. 'Blessing' and 'thanksgiving' are the same word in Aramaic which was translated *eulogia* in Hellenistic Jewish circles and *eucharistia* in Gentile circles.

But in all the liturgies the actions have been reduced to four.
(1) The celebrant takes bread and wine (at the offertory).
(2) He gives thanks over both (in the great eucharistic prayer).
(3) He breaks the bread (at the Fraction after the eucharistic
prayer and prior to distribution). (4) He receives the bread
and wine himself and distributes to the other ministers and
people.

What has happened is that the blessing or thanksgiving
uttered over the bread (which was quite a short one at Jewish
meals and may have been so in early celebrations of the Lord's
Supper, i.e., the combination of *agape* and Eucharist) has been
combined with the longer thanksgiving prayer uttered over the
cup. This involves the postponement of the Fraction or breaking of the bread, until after the eucharistic prayer in preparation for distribution. All this was a natural and obvious
adjustment for the Church to make when it separated the
Eucharist from the *agape;* and the fact that it is found in the
same manner throughout the Church, both East and West,
makes it fairly certain that the adjustment took place in very
early times, probably in the apostolic period; though it may
not have happened everywhere at the same time. This is the
common factor which gave unity to the Eucharists of the
universal Church. The eucharistic prayer itself might vary
from place to place and from celebrant to celebrant, extempore prayer being still the norm in the second century and
still permissible in the fifth and later. But the basic structure
everywhere was the same; so that when in A.D. 154 Polycarp,
Bishop of Smyrna, visited Pope Anicetus at Rome, the latter
could invite him to celebrate the Eucharist without any fear of
his people being offended or embarrassed by any unfamiliar
rite. Indeed the Syrian *Didaskalia* of the third century makes
such an invitation to a visiting bishop obligatory.[1]

This four action shape is in a measure obscured for us by
the insertion into the eucharistic prayer of all the liturgies

---

[1] Jungmann, op. cit., i, p. 32.

(except the East Syrian *Liturgy of Addai and Mari*. See pp. 70ff.) of the narrative of the Institution which then becomes a miniature drama within the greater drama of the fourfold action[1] giving it its meaning and its authority as done according to the command of Christ. Those of us who are heirs of the Western Liturgical heritage (through the Churches of the Reformation) are particularly liable to be misled by the fact that the West came to regard the recital of the Words of Institution as effecting consecration, instead of regarding consecration as taking place in the whole process of setting apart with thanksgiving.   Still further confusion occurred when in the late Middle Ages a preliminary fraction was often added at the works 'He brake it' in imitation of our Lord's action at the Last Supper and to emphasize the symbolic interpretation of the breaking of bread as representing Christ's death. The Reformers (e.g. in the Anglican rite) tended to adopt this subsidiary fraction of later origin and to discard the original one after the eucharistic prayer and thus disrupt the primitive four action shape and obscure the primary purpose of the Fraction, namely distribution. The *Order for the Lord's Supper* of the Church of South India has rightly restored the shape by putting the Fraction back in its proper place.

But we have not yet accounted for the completion of the structure of the liturgy in the ministry of the Word which preceded the eucharistic act. In Chapter 2 we have seen the debt which the early Church owed to the synagogue in its worship, and that the synagogue worship was built up around the reading of Scripture which was followed by a sermon and prayer.   When the Church became separated from the synagogue—possibly as early as A.D. 44 in Palestine, as a result of persecution, and not long after their foundation in the Pauline Churches—it evidently continued the same type of worship, though the ordered pattern of the worship of the

---

1 Like the little play performed by the players in *Hamlet*. But do not press this illustration too far !

synagogue was sometimes strained, as at Corinth (1 Cor. 14), by those who spoke with tongues and prophesied. Whether, as some scholars think, this pentecostal worship took place as part of the same meeting of the *Ecclesia* as that in which it had come together to celebrate the Lord's Supper (1 Cor. 11) is debatable. In 1 Cor. 11 Paul rebukes the Corinthian Christians for not waiting for the humbler members of the Church (presumably the slaves who had to work late) before partaking of food, so that when the latter came there was nothing left for them. If the Lord's Supper had been preceded by a lengthy meeting, including psalms, hymns, prophecies and ecstatic utterances with their accompanying interpretations, the slaves would have had to arrive very late indeed to miss the final eucharistic act. It is probable therefore that at this time in Corinth there were still two distinct and separate types of worship.[1] Paul's Eucharist, however, at Troas on the first day of the week is a sign that he himself, at any rate in the latter part of his ministry, had begun to join the two services together and that the classical pattern of a service of the Word preceding the Eucharist is beginning to emerge. Its establishment must have been early for it to have become universal in the ancient liturgies. If the opening of the scroll and the hymns of adoration uttered by the triumphant saints in the Book of Revelation and the culmination of the book in the marriage feast of the Lamb are intended to show that the eucharistic worship of the Church on earth corresponds to the worship of heaven, then we have an indication that this pattern was taking shape in the Churches which John knew at the end of the first century.

FROM THE SECOND CENTURY TO THE FOURTH

When we pass from the apostolic age to the beginning of the second century our evidence is slight. The first document we must consider is a pagan one, the letter of the Younger

[1] C. F. D. Moule (in *Worship in the N. T.*, ch. IV), argues that vigorous non-sacramental worship took place in the N.T. period alongside the meetings for the Eucharist.

Pliny, who was Governor of Bithynia about A.D. 111-13, to the Emperor Trajan, about some Christians he had arrested and examined. He wrote in the course of it :

> They [the Christians] asserted that the substance of their fault or error was that they were in the habit of meeting on a fixed day before daylight and reciting responsively among themselves a hymn to Christ as a god, and that they bound themselves by an oath not to commit any crime but to abstain from theft, robbery and adultery, that they should not break their word or deny a deposit when called upon to pay it. When they had performed this it was their custom to depart and to meet together again for a meal, but of a common and harmless kind. They said they had even given up doing this since the promulgation of my edict, by which, in accordance with your commands, I had forbidden the existence of clubs.

Here we get an objective glimpse of the Church at worship under persecution from the point of view of a persecutor. Pliny, like many a colonial governor, faced with the customs of a subject people, probably little understood what it was all about, and no doubt the Christians themselves concealed as much as they could from a hostile pagan the details of their worship, particularly of the Eucharist. But if the word translated 'hymn' above really means 'religious formula', as it probably does, then here we may have a reference to the versicles and responses at the beginning of the eucharistic prayer ('Lift up your hearts', etc.) and the prayer itself which may have contained responses of the people. The oath to avoid certain sins might be the beginning of the 'fencing of the table' by which the baptized who participated in the Eucharist were examined and notorious sinners excluded.[1] We may compare the injunction in the *Didache:*

> Every Lord's Day when you come together,[1] break bread

[1] Or it may refer to the renunciation of sin in Baptism.

and give thanks (or 'celebrate the eucharist') after confessing your sins, that your sacrifice may be pure.

We may conjecture that the word 'sacrifice' here refers to the Eucharist.

To return to the Christians of Bithynia, apart from mentioning the responsive hymn or rite, they, of course, were silent before the Roman official about the eucharistic mysteries celebrated before dawn, but had no compunction about giving details of the less sacred *agape* held later in the day, perhaps in the evening; and it did not much matter their having discontinued the latter in obedience to government orders. The 'fixed day' must be Sunday.

Justin

Our next document is the *Apology* of Justin Martyr, written in Rome about A.D. 140 to the Emperor Antoninus Pius. It contains two accounts of the Eucharist as celebrated at Rome in his time. The former is that of the baptismal Eucharist to which we have already referred in Chapter 3. The latter describes the normal gathering (*synaxis*) of the faithful on Sunday:

On the day called the day of the Sun there is a meeting together of all who live in cities or in the country, and the memoirs of the Apostles and the writings of the prophets are read as time allows. Then when the reader has ended the president exhorts and admonishes us in his address to conform to this excellent teaching. After this we all rise together and offer prayers. . . . When our prayers are ended bread is brought up and wine and water, and the president offers prayers and thanksgiving (*eucharistias*) according to his ability and the people respond with the Amen. The distribution follows and the reception by each of the

---

[1] Compare with the Greek word *synachthentes* the word *synaxis* = 'coming together' which at an early date became almost a technical term for the assembly of the whole local *ecclesia* for eucharistic worship. We shall have occasion to use this word again.

elements which have been set apart with thanksgiving. These are also sent to those who are absent by the hands of the deacons. Of those who are prosperous and willing each gives according to his own resolve, and the collection is entrusted to the president. He it is who gives assistance to orphans, widows, those in want through sickness or any other cause, prisoners and foreigners staying in our midst. In short he looks after all who are in need.

In addition to this account and the previous one concerning the baptismal Eucharist there are references in the *Dialogue with Trypho*. If we bring together all these references we get the following outline of the service :

1. Readings from the memoirs of the Apostles ('which are called Gospels').
2. Sermon by the 'president'.
3. Intercessions for all men, said standing.
4. The kiss of peace (mentioned in the account of the baptismal Eucharist).
5. Presentation to the president of bread and a cup of wine and water.
6. Praise, prayer and thanksgiving (i.e., the eucharistic prayer) offered by the president extempore and addressed to the Father through the name of the Son and of the Holy Spirit.
7. The response of all the people to this prayer : 'Amen'.
8. The administration of the bread and the cup to the people by the deacons who also take them to those who are absent.
9. The collection of alms is only mentioned after the account of the service and perhaps took place at the end. It is administered for the relief of the needy by the president.

The word *eucharistia* denotes the rite, as already earlier in the second century in the epistles of Ignatius. 'We do not receive,' Justin says, 'these (elements) as common bread and common drink; but just as Jesus Christ our Saviour was made flesh by the word of God and took both flesh and blood for our salvation so also the food which has been set apart by thanksgiving (literally : "the food thanked for") through the word of prayer (or "the prayer of the Word") which is from him, by which our blood and flesh are nourished through digestion, is both flesh and blood of that Jesus who was made flesh.'

Elsewhere he says that 'the bread of the Eucharist' is offered as 'a memorial of the Passion', and like the author of the *Didache* he quotes Malachi 1. 11 with reference to it. There is therefore doubtless a doctrine of offering and of the eucharistic sacrifice; but the main emphasis in Justin's account is (*a*) on the corporateness of the rite (everyone coming together to the common worship, all standing together for prayer and, above all, the whole congregation responding 'Amen'; (*b*) *eucharistia* = thanksgiving, a word which as noun or verb is repeated again and again. It is by the thanksgiving prayer that the bread and wine become the body and blood of Christ, though there may be in addition the concept of the Word (Logos) descending upon them, if it is right to translate one phrase quoted above as 'the prayer of the Word which is from him (God the Father)' rather than as 'the word of prayer which is from him (Christ, who first offered the prayer of thanksgiving over the bread and wine)'. This would agree with the theology which we shall find in the eucharistic prayer of Sarapion, and it is significant that there was close intercourse between the Church of Rome and the Church of Alexandria.

Although Ignatius of Antioch at the beginning of the century had written, 'Let that be held a valid Eucharist which is under the bishop or him to whom he commits it', Rome had been late in adopting monarchical episcopacy. However, it is generally assumed that 'the president' in Justin's account refers to the bishop.

Probably the meeting place was a house which had been put at the disposal of the Christian congregation. Some churches in Rome still bear the names of wealthy Christians (Clement, Caecilia, etc.) who owned houses on the sites where the churches are now built. Ruins of a private house, which was transformed, so the inscription relates, into a church in A.D. 232 have been excavated in the old Roman garrison of Dura-Europos in Mesopotamia. The adaptation was apparently made by removing an inner wall and so making two rooms into one assembly hall.

Hippolytus

Another document of surpassing interest comes to us also from Rome. It is the work of the Roman presbyter Hippolytus and was known for long under the title, *The Egyptian Church Order;* but its proper name is *The Apostolic Tradition.* It was probably written about A.D. 215, but the author claims that it represents the tradition of his church of at least a generation earlier. We have already had occasion to refer to his description in it of the baptismal rite and we shall later return to his ordination prayers. It is in connexion with ordination that he gives us in full what is so important for us at this point in our study, the only extant eucharistic prayer composed before the Council of Nicaea which has not been revised by later generations.

After a new bishop has been consecrated and acclaimed with the cry 'He is worthy', the deacons bring up the gifts of bread and wine. Accompanied by all the presbyters, the bishops lay their hands over the gifts and say together the eucharistic prayer. This is an example of the primitive practice of concelebration. The prayer is as follows :

> The Lord be with you : And with thy spirit.
> Lift up your hearts : We lift them up unto the Lord.
> Let us give thanks unto the Lord : It is meet and right.
> We give thanks to thee, O God, through thy beloved

Servant Jesus Christ whom in the last times thou didst send to be the Saviour, Redeemer and Messenger of thy will. He is thy Word inseparable from thee; through him thou didst create everything and in him thou wast well pleased.

Thou didst send him into the Virgin's womb, and being conceived within her he was incarnate and revealed as thy Son, being born of the Holy Spirit and the Virgin. And fulfilling thy will and acquiring for thee a holy people, he stretched forth his hands when he suffered that he might deliver from sufferings those who have believed in thee.

And when he was betrayed to the passion of his own free will, that he might abolish death, break the chains of the devil and tread down hell and give light to the righteous and establish the time of the end and reveal the resurrection, he took bread and giving thanks to thee said : 'Take, eat; this is my body which will be broken for you.' In the same way also, the cup, saying : 'This is my blood which is poured out for you. When you do this, you make my memorial.'

Remembering therefore his death and resurrection we offer to thee the bread and the cup giving thanks to thee that thou hast deemed us worthy to stand in thy presence and minister to thee.

And we beseech thee that thou wouldst send thy Holy Spirit on the oblation of thy holy Church. Do thou gather into one and grant to all the saints who partake the fulness of the Holy Spirit for the confirmation of faith in truth that we may praise and glorify thee through thy servant Jesus Christ, through whom be glory to thee and honour, to the Father and to the Son with the Holy Spirit in thy holy Church, both now and unto the ages of ages. Amen.

The 'harvest festival' character of the primitive offertory is illustrated by the provision made after this for a blessing of oil, cheese and olives. We have already noticed the special

administration of milk, honey and water to the newly baptized
at their first communion.

As Jungmann observes, it would be a mistake to regard
Hippolytus' eucharistic prayer as *the* Roman Mass of the third
century, pure and simple. This would be contrary to what we
know from other sources of the development of the liturgy at
this time. There is no fixed form of words but only a common
framework which the celebrant fills out in his own manner.
Indeed Hippolytus himself makes this clear when he writes :
'There is absolutely no necessity for the bishop to use the
precise wording which we have given... Rather each man
should pray according to his ability.' And he adds that the
prayer may be either extempore or according to a set form,
provided it is orthodox. But when later *The Apostolic
Tradition* was translated into Arabic and Ethiopic, the notion
of fixity and uniformity had come in and the words 'there is
absolutely no necessity' were changed to 'it is absolutely
necessary' ! That this particular prayer is Hippolytus' own
composition is indicated by several parallels to phrases and
teaching in his other writings.

A point to notice about the prayer is its brevity and com-
pactness and the neat literary manner in which the remembrance of redemption in Christ passes on into the narrative of
the institution. Indeed Christ's incarnation, and redemption
through him, are the predominant themes of the thanksgiving,
mention of creation being passed over in half a sentence. In
this the prayer is unlike other ancient eucharistic prayers of
which we know which are more loosely constructed and long-
winded. Hippolytus may have been consciously reacting against
these diffuse prayers, derived as many of them were from
synagogue worship, and we do not know whether his omission
of the *Sanctus* (Holy, Holy, Holy) is because it did not belong
to the Roman tradition of this time or because he thought the
prayer would be more straightforward and to the point with-

out it.[1] There is evidence in 1 Clement that the *Sanctus* was known in Rome more than a century earlier, though not necessarily then used in the eucharistic prayer. However, the parallels noted between Hippolytus and the accounts of Justin Martyr[2] show that we are dealing with a prayer that, in spite of its individual characteristics, belonged to the primitive Roman tradition.

We may note the inclusion in the prayer of an *Epiklesis* (invocation of the Holy Spirit). Most scholars agree that this is genuine here and not an interpolation, in spite of its absence in one fifth-century quotation of the prayer. There is no reason why Hippolytus should not have included such a prayer for the Holy Spirit, even though it is absent from the later Roman Canon (eucharistic prayer). In any case it is not, like the later Eastern forms of *Epiklesis,* a formula of consecration of the bread and wine, which are thought of as being filled with the Spirit. Rather it is a prayer for the offering Church in its 'oblation' that it may be united in worship. 'It is in fact a prayer for the communicants.'[3]

It is also to be noted that Hippolytus' prayer contains an *Anamnesis* (memorial) of the death and resurrection of Christ with which is connected the offering of the bread and cup. All other orthodox liturgies have a similar *Anamnesis* at the same point after the recital of the Words of Institution, and it is likely that this belongs to the earliest tradition.

Owing to the historical circumstances—the dispute between Hippolytus and Callistus who became Bishop of Rome and in opposition to whom he set himself up as anti-pope—

---

[1] Dix is of opinion that the use of the Preface and *Sanctus* first developed in Alexandria and spread from there to other parts of Christendom. The suggestion has, however, been recently put forward by Professor E. C. Ratcliff that the *Sanctus* formed the culmination of the eucharistic prayer immediately before the Fraction. In this case Hippolytus' omission of it would be explained by the fact that it was said or sung by the whole congregation and not by the celebrant alone.

[2] See G. Dix, *The Shape of the Liturgy,* p. 159.

[3] J. H. Srawley, *The Early History of the Liturgy,* p. 70.

Hippolytus' *Apostolic Tradition* was almost entirely forgotten in Rome and the West, but was of great influence in Egypt and Syria as representing the primitive Roman tradition. It survived mainly in Coptic, Arabic and Ethiopian translatons and its eucharistic prayer is still found in the Ethiopian liturgy today. This is a good example of the borrowing of liturgical forms which is a feature of the early centuries, particularly borrowing by provincial Churches from a metropolitan Church of authority and influence.

We have evidence for the influence of the great sees in the legislation for and control of worship from the fourth century onwards. The two centres which were particularly influential in the East were Alexandria and Antioch, and it was as a result of the adoption of the respective ways of worship of these and other preponderant centres by neighbouring Churches that the different local liturgies began to acquire their fixed form.

But standardization took centuries to complete, as is shown by the fact that from the end of the fourth century survive two collections of liturgical texts, one coming from Egypt and the other from Syria, the spheres of influence of Alexandria and Antioch respectively, in which the orders for the Eucharist differ considerably from the liturgies which were later established.

The first of these is the *Euchologion* (Prayer Book) of Sarapion who was bishop of Thmuis, a little town in Lower Egypt, between A.D. 339 and 362 and a friend of Athanasius and Anthony. The manuscript of this book was found in a monastery on Mount Athos in 1894. We must not think of it as like modern published prayer books, but rather as the bishop's own private collection of the prayers which he required for use. There is no very coherent order about them, and rubrics are lacking. Many thousands of such episcopal note-books have no doubt disappeared for ever, as this one nearly did.

The eucharistic prayer is probably, like Hippolytus' prayer, an individual composition by a local bishop, very likely Sarapion himself. It varies considerably from the later *Liturgy of St. Mark* in which eventually was standardized the main liturgical tradition of Egypt at its centre in Alexandria. But, while Sarapion differs elsewhere from *Mark,* in the Preface and *Sanctus* they are at one. Sarapion has a long address of adoration to God before the Preface which links up better with the passage following the *Sanctus* than with the Preface. It is probable therefore that the Bishop of Thmuis, as belonging to the province of Alexandria and owing respect to its Patriarch, took the Alexandrian form of the Preface and *Sanctus* and inserted it in his local rite. He has also rather surprisingly borrowed from the *Didache,* thinking perhaps that it was apostolic in authorship. He takes the passage, 'as this bread has been scattered on the mountains...' and inserts it into the narrative of the Institution between the words concerning the bread and the cup. We have already observed that this kind of borrowing was common in the early centuries.

The influence of Alexandria can also be seen in the Greek rhetorical style with which the prayer is adorned at the beginning. It piles up epithets to the glory of God in the manner common in the Eastern liturgies. The opening address (before the Preface) is of more than 200 words. Characteristic of the Greek theology of this time are the negative attributes of God, 'unsearchable, ineffable, incomprehensible by any created substance'. There is a clear concern to exalt the Son and guard against Arianism, but in contrast to Hippolytus, the remembrance of redemption through Christ is absent and only a very brief remembrance of the Passion is found in close conjunction with the Words of Institution. The offering of the elements comes before the narrative of the Institution :

Full is the heaven, full is the earth of thy excellent glory, Lord of Hosts. Fill also this sacrifice with thy power and participation; for to thee have we offered this living sacrifice, this bloodless oblation. To thee have we offered this bread, the likeness of the body of the only begotten One.

And after the first Word of Institution :

> Wherefore, we also, making the likeness of the death, have offered the bread, and beseech thee through this sacrifice, O God of truth, to be reconciled to us all and to be merciful . . .

And after the second Word of Institution :

> Wherefore we have also offered the cup presenting a likeness of the blood.

The words 'fill with thy power' may be simply a rhetorical re-echoing of the word 'full' at the beginning of the sentence rather than a theory of consecration as effected by an imparting of divine power (*dynamis*) to the bread and the wine, as has sometimes been supposed.

There follows an *Epiklesis* which, however, differs from those of the later liturgies in its invocation of the Logos rather than of the Spirit :

> O God of truth, let thy holy Word come upon this bread, that the bread may become the body of the Word, and upon this cup that the cup may become the blood of the Truth . . .[1]

This accords with Alexandrian doctrine concerning the Logos and is characteristically Eastern in its concept of the *Epiklesis* as the prayer for consecration of the elements. The elements have been offered before this in the prayers quoted above, but only as the 'likeness'[2] of the body and blood which they have in view of their being taken up into the eucharistic action. They are not thought of as *becoming* the body and blood of Christ until the Logos descends upon them in answer to the prayers of the Church.

[1] Translation by W. D. Maxwell, *An Outline of Christian Worship*.

[2] Some scholars, however, argue that the Greek word translated 'likeness' means more than the English word 'likeness' and should be translated 'representation'. This also applies to the Latin word *figura* (figure) found in the parallel passage in the earliest form of the Roman Mass.

The prayer ends with intercessions for the living and the dead (presupposing a reading of their names) and for those who offer the particular Eucharist being celebrated. These intercessions within the eucharistic prayer are absent from Hippolytus' prayer, and Justin also implies that intercessions belong to an earlier part of the rite. Sarapion's Prayer Book has some intercessions elsewhere which contain a repeated doxology characteristic of the fourth century in which God the Father is praised 'through Christ in the Holy Spirit'. But whether these intercessions belonged to the earlier part of the Eucharist is uncertain.

In any case these intercessions within the eucharistic prayer are probably a third- or fourth-century addition to the prayer. The reason for this innovation is a belief, which finds expression both in East and West, that intercessions in the presence of the blessed sacrament are of particular efficacy. For instance in the *Liturgy of St. James* (see below) it is said of these intercessions : 'This is the greatest aid to souls of those for whom the intercession is made in the presence of the holy and most dread sacrifice.' These very words go back to the catechetical lectures of Cyril of Jerusalem who also compares the eucharistic sacrifice to a crown offered to a king by his subjects to obtain relaxation of punishment for others. In the West we have a letter of a fifth-century Pope, Innocent I, which stresses the importance of praying 'in the presence of the sacred mysteries' for those who offer their gifts, i.e., within the eucharistic prayer.

Altogether this eucharistic prayer is interesting not for any liturgical merit which it has, nor because it was a liturgy which was in any way the parent of later liturgies; but because it shows the kind of individuality which local rites everywhere no doubt had in style and theology at this time. A full text will be found in J. Wordsworth, *Bishop Sarapion's Prayer Book,* and full translations of the eucharistic prayer in Maxwell and Dix, opp. cit.

The Apostolic Constitutions

The other document from this period is *The Apostolic Constitutions* which is written in the name of Clement, Bishop of Rome at the end of the first century, but is really a product of the late fourth century. Book VIII of *The Apostolic Constitutions* as a whole is mainly a revision of *The Apostolic Tradition* of Hippolytus, but it contains a eucharistic liturgy which is little influenced by Hippolytus' draft. This is the so-called *Clementine Liturgy*. There is a summary of a similar rite (possibly from an earlier source) in Book II, which implies the reading of a large number of lections from the Law, the historical books, Job and the Wisdom books, the Prophets, Acts, Epistles and Gospels. These are followed by the direction :

> Then let the presbyters exhort the people, one at a time, but not all of them; and last of all the bishop, as befits the captain of a ship.

The liturgy in Book VIII begins with only four or five lections, two from the Old Testament and two or three from the New Testament, and is followed by a homily from the new bishop who is apparently consecrated after the lections, as in *The Apostolic Tradition;* though the author, unlike Hippolytus, does not give us the formula of consecration. Then follows a series of dismissals of different groups of non-Communicants—the catechumens, energumens (i.e., those possessed with devils), the 'illuminated' (i.e., those nearly ready for baptism), and the penitents. Each group comes forward in turn at the bidding of a deacon who says a litany of intercession for each group, and the people respond : 'Lord have mercy.' Each litany is followed by a prayer of blessing for the group concerned, given by the bishop, and then the deacon bids the group go forth in peace.

These dismissals are followed by the prayers of the faithful —a larger litany for the Church and the world, followed by a long prayer by the bishop.

The ministry of the Word (The 'Liturgy of the Cate-chumens', as it was called) which is the preparatory part of the service is now ended, and only the faithful (the baptized who are not under discipline) are left in church to celebrate the Eucharist. They begin with the ancient symbol of their brotherhood in Christ, the Kiss of Peace ('Let the clergy kiss the bishop, the laymen the laymen and the women the women').

After this the colourful rubrics reveal a mounting intensity of concentration.

> Let the children stand near the platform,[1] and let a deacon supervise them that they be not disorderly. And let other deacons go around the men and the women and inspect them that there be no disturbance and no one make signs or whisper or slumber. And let the deacons be stationed at the men's doors and the sub-deacons at those of the women, so that no one of the faithful may go out nor the door be opened during the time of the *Anaphora* [eucharistic prayer].

After the washing of hands administered by a deacon to the bishop and presbyters, a deacon 'fences the table' by forbidding the presence of any who are debarred from partici-pating. This includes 'anyone who is at enmity with anyone

[1] This was an oblong platform placed lengthways in the centre of the nave with the bishop's throne at the western end of it facing east-wards towards the altar at the eastern end of the church. Another passage in *The Apostolic Constitutions* mentions the presbyters seated on either side of the bishop and the deacons standing by. From this platform or pulpit the first part of the service (the Liturgy of the Catechumens) was read. The men came in by the eastern door on the south side (as in a synagogue) and sat in front of the platform, the women by the western door on the south side and sat behind. It was no doubt convenient to have the children on either side of the platform between the men and the women. See B. Minchin, *The Celebration of the Eucharist facing the People*. Were the primitive wooden churches of Kerala of this pattern? Un-fortunately the heavy rainfall was not favourable to their survival, and they have perished without a trace; but the Syrian origin of these Churches leads us to conjecture that they were.

and anyone who is a hypocrite' as well as those who have already been dismissed.

All is now prepared for the offering of gifts which are brought by the deacons to the bishop at the altar. We then get a description of the bishop with 'the presbyters standing on the right hand and on the left, like disciples grouped around their teacher'. 'Meanwhile 'two deacons on either side of the altar hold fans of fine parchment, peacock's feathers or linen and gently whisk away the flies that they settle not on the vessels'. The bishop surrounded by his presbyters 'puts on a splendid vestment and, after making the sign of the cross on his forehead', begins the eucharistic prayer.[1]

This commences with the usual dialogue between celebrant and people, including the *Sursum corda* (Lift up your hearts).[2]

A very long preface follows giving thanks for God's providence as manifested in creation and the call of Israel and recalling all the main events in Genesis and Exodus. It is followed by the *Sanctus* which makes a division between the commemoration of the old covenant and the new; for the prayer then proceeds to recall the mystery of the Incarnation and redemption with equally detailed reference to the events of the Gospels.

We must regard this lengthy opening as the composition of the author or redactor and not part of a rite that was ever regularly in use. The fiction is maintained in the rubrics that

[1] From the study of ruined churches in north Syria it is clear that there was no room for the celebrant to stand behind the table facing the people as in the Greek and Roman basilicas. Churches faced East (not West, as did the basilicas) and the celebrant and people both faced in this direction. This was the posture which eventually superseded throughout Christendom the Greek and Roman basilican manner of celebrating. See B. Minchin, *The Celebration of the Eucharist Facing the People*.

[2] The first greeting and response, as in all Eastern liturgies except the Egyptian, is:
> The grace of God Almighty, the love of our Lord Jesus Christ and the fellowship of the Holy Spirit be with you all:
> And with thy spirit.

In the West the greeting is: The Lord be with you . . .

the Apostles taught this liturgy to Clement and the idea no
doubt is that such heroes of the faith must have uttered ideal
prayers of heroic length. In any case the eucharistic rite was
still fluid at this time and the intention of the composer may
have been to provide a quarry from which celebrants could
obtain material for the free composition of their own prayers.

But after this opening (which itself is no doubt an expansion
of a traditional one) the eucharistic prayer is closely similar in
structure and content to later liturgies of Syrian origin and
may be regarded as representative of the eucharistic tradition
from which they emerged. The order, though not the wording,
is the same as that of Hippolytus, and the influence of his
draft may here be discerned.

The commemoration of the Incarnation and Redemption
(already mentioned) leads to the Narrative of the Institution.
This is followed by an *Anamnesis* which recalls Christ's second
coming as well as his death and resurrection and includes the
offering of the bread and the cup.

The *Epiklesis* (Prayer for the Holy Spirit) is of the developed
Eastern type :

> We beseech thee to look favourably upon these gifts which
> lie before thee, O God who needeth nothing, and manifest
> thy good pleasure towards them for the honour of thy
> Christ and send upon this sacrifice thy Holy Spirit, the
> witness of the passion of our Lord Jesus, that he might
> reveal this bread as the body of Christ and this cup as the
> blood of Christ and that all we who partake of it may be
> strengthened in godliness ...

An intercessory prayer of ten sections follows and the whole
is concluded with the doxology and the Amen of the people.

From the devotions preparatory to Communion the Lord's
Prayer is missing, though it seems to have become universal
not very much later as a communion prayer. There are
bidding prayers by the deacon and a prayer by the bishop,
after which the bishop says :

Holy things for holy people.

And the people reply with the hymn :

> There is one holy, one Lord Jesus Christ who is blessed
> for evermore to the glory of God the Father. Amen.
> Glory to God in the highest and on earth peace and good-
> will amongst men.
> Hosanna to the Son of David.
> Blessed is he that cometh in the name of the Lord.
> The Lord God has revealed him : Hosanna in the highest.

The bread and the cup are administered by the bishop and
deacon respectively with the words 'The body of Christ' and
'The blood of Christ', to which each recipient responds,
'Amen', the women and children receiving Communion
immediately after the clergy, choir and instrumentalists, and
the men last. The people are then called to thanksgiving by
the deacon. Finally, after two prayers by the bishop, the
deacon dismisses them saying, 'Depart in peace'.

The value of this and the previous liturgical texts which we
have examined is that, owing to their neglect for centuries,
they have remained unrevised and free from the later accretions both liturgical and theological which we find in the rites
which became established in the various provinces of the
Church. To take an illustration from architecture, a ruined
city such as Fatehpur in India, or a ruined abbey such as that
of Melrose near the Scottish border, is in either case purer in
its architectural style than if it had continued in use by later
generations and received the accretions of their building. Both
the city and the abbey, if they had continued in use, would
have had the advantage of being 'alive' in the sense of being
associated with the activities of living people, instead of
belonging only to a dead past. Similarly the rites of Christendom which have continued in use to the present day are alive,
as these ones to which we are now directing our attention
are not. But just as we value ancient ruins both for their

architectural and historical interest, so too these ancient
liturgical documents are of value to us as revealing the form
and spirit of the early Church's worship which became
obscured in later ages.

What impresses us in this liturgy of *The Apostolic Constitutions?* Firstly its firm basis in Scripture and the declaration
of the Word of God. Not only is much time devoted to hearing
the Bible read and to preaching based upon it, but the
eucharistic prayer itself is replete with scriptural allusions
mostly of a straightforward unallegorical character.

Secondly, we observe the congregational character of the
service. There is no suggestion of ministers withdrawn from
the people conducting the rite while the people passively look
on or engage in devotions more or less dissociated from the
main action, such as we find in medieval worship. On the
contrary everyone has a part to play, even the children, who
are mentioned three times in the rubrics. In fact, while the
liturgy is one, it is also true to say that every order in the
Church has its 'liturgy' to perform. 'Liturgy' means 'the
people's work' and in the Christian sense of the word it is the
service of the people of God rendered to him. The celebrant,
to be sure, has a pre-eminent part to play; but he cannot
perform it without the constant assistance of the deacons in
directing the service and leading the people, who also have
their indispensable responsibility in demonstrating their unity
in the kiss of peace, making their offerings, singing the hymns
under the leadership of the choir and rendering the responses,
particularly the significant 'Amen'.

Thirdly, the rite still retains something of its primitive
simplicity. There is, of course, an imposing array of ministers
surrounding the bishop who puts on a beautiful garment for
the eucharistic prayer, and the eucharistic prayer itself is
composed in the grand manner; but there is as yet nothing in
the ceremonial to outshine the central action and no secondary
devotions of the minister or of the people to distract attention
from it. Rather, the concentration on what is being done in

the Eucharist from the offertory to the communion is intense, and the whole congregation is directed towards it. We know from other sources that, even in the third century when the Church was still liable to persecution, Christians in the cities adorned such church buildings as they had with some splendour and had a surprising wealth of gold and silver vessels and other ornaments. An array of this kind is presupposed by this liturgy, appropriate, as it was regarded, for the bishop's celebration.

No doubt there were much simpler services in the house churches which were universal in the first two centuries and the norm in the early part of the third. Services in the outlying rural congregations, even if they possessed a church building, would also inevitably be of a more modest character. It is one of the unfortunate gaps in liturgical studies that we know little or nothing of the manner of this simpler worship, all the texts which survive having been composed for the bishop's service at the centre of his diocese to which the rural presbyter eventually conformed, even though this more imposing rite was not really suited to his use. But in this rite of the fourth century, belonging though it does to the splendid worship of a large congregation, we have not yet got to the stage when the honours due to the emperor at court in Constantinople are paid to the sacramental elements, and the bishop and his ministers treated in the ceremonial according to their rank in imperial officialdom. This is what happened in the Byzantine rites (see below) and in the stational masses of sixth- and seventh-century popes in the basilicas of Rome. In *The Apostolic Constitutions,* however, the fans waved by the deacons over the chalice still appear to have only a utilitarian function.

TOWARDS UNIFORMITY IN THE EAST

The picture of Christian worship which we get from the available evidence up to the middle of the fourth century is that of a variety of local rites and customs. In the East,[1] however, a process of unification began under the patronage of the imperial court at Byzantium (Constantinople). The aims of the emperors were no doubt in some measure political. A Church whose worship was unified in conformity with that of the capital city would make for a unified empire. But this urge for unity reached beyond the bounds of the Roman empire, as is shown by the mission sent about A.D. 354 by the Emperor Constantius to the churches in South Arabia, Ethiopia, Ceylon and India. On the west coast of India, where the ancestors of the Syrian Christians of today were already established, the leader of the mission, Theophilus the Indian, 'reformed many things which were not rightly done among them; for they heard the reading of the Gospel in a sitting posture and did other things which were repugnant to the divine law; and having reformed everything according to the holy usage, as was acceptable to God, he also confirmed the dogma of the Church'.[2]

Whether the practices of which Theophilus disapproved were actual errors which had crept into this outlying church, or whether they were all harmless deviations from the use of other churches, such as the sitting for the reading of the Gospel, which he mentions, we do not know. But probably the kind of worship which he tried to establish would be similar to that set forth in *The Apostolic Constitutions* which, as we have seen, belongs to this period. It is evident that this and similar efforts had little lasting effect outside the empire where the churches continued largely in their local heritage of worship. Within the Empire too, the move towards uniformity was to be checked by dissensions within the Church not unrelated to the social and racial tensions of Syria and Egypt. It was only the worship of the Greek-speaking Church which conformed finally to Byzantium.

[1] The history of Liturgy in the West was different. See ch. 6.
[2] Quoted from L. W. Brown, *The Indian Christians of St. Thomas,* p. 67. See his footnote for the evidence.

CHAPTER 5

THE LITURGIES OF THE EAST

BYZANTIUM

EVEN in the latter part of the third century during the 'second long peace' of the Church from the edict of Gallienus (260) to the outbreak of the last persecution under Diocletian (303), Christian worship had been able to emerge from the secrecy of private houses and the catacombs, and churches of some magnificence had been built in the cities. The modest splendour which we find in the Liturgy of *The Apostolic Constitutions* no doubt dates from this period. But the battle of the Milvian Bridge (312) in which Constantine, the first Christian emperor, was victorious marked the beginning of a new epoch in the Church's worship, as well as in other aspects of her life. In particular the emperor's own example gave incentive to the widespread building of more splendid churches and the development of a public worship of royal magnificence. At the same time in the eastern empire, where the Church tended to be subservient to the imperial court, imperial patronage soon began to favour uniformity of worship as well as of doctrine, as a means of uniting the Empire. We have seen one instance of the imperial influence extending beyond the bounds of the empire, even as far as India. Within the Greek-speaking Church which remained orthodox this uniformity had triumphed by the seventh century, and the two rites known as the Byzantine rites everywhere superseded the older rites. In Russia and neighbouring Slav countries they were translated into Old Slavonic and became the use of the Church there. They are the *Liturgy of St. Basil,* the longer of the two rites, which is only used on certain days of the year, and the *Liturgy of St. Chrysostom,* which is the normal eucharistic rite.

From one point of view this was the triumphant culmination of Eastern worship; but in several respects it marked the
beginning of its decline.

In the first place, the enforcement of uniformity from
Byzantium and the suppression of the local rites in Eastern
catholicism meant that no new factor emerged in Eastern
worship from the seventh century onwards with the result that
hardly anything has changed since then.

Secondly, though *eucharistia* (thanksgiving) is still present
in the later liturgies, there comes in a more gloomy and
pessimistic emphasis as a result of the increased consciousness
of sin and enhanced reverence in the presence of the great
eucharistic mystery. Phrases such as 'thy lowly, sinful and
unworthy slaves' creep in, and at the *Epiklesis* the Deacon says
to the people : 'My beloved, how fearful is this moment and
how dreadful is this time when the Holy Spirit descends from
heaven, from the heights above, and dwells upon this Holy
Qurbana (Eucharist) and sanctifies it' (Syrian *Liturgy of St.
James*). No wonder that the laity were afraid to approach
the holy table, and reception of communion declined. One
reason for this was the controversy with the Arians which had
led the orthodox to stress the divinity of Christ and the
fearsomeness of his divine judgment.

In addition the partition between the sanctuary and the
nave became more pronounced. The railings which divided
the one from the other became a solid wall, the *ikonostasis*
which hides the eucharistic celebration from the people.[1] The
interposition of this screen made necessary the two processions
from the sanctuary through the nave and back again to the
sanctuary which are characteristic of the Byzantine rite. The
first is the 'Little Entrance' before the reading of the Gospel
in which the Gospel book is carried accompanied by lights,

[1] Dix suggests that this development may have been due to the
practice in the East of receiving the offerings of the people in the
sacristy beforehand, whereas in the West, where the rite has always
remained visible, they were received at the chancel at the offertory,
But this point still awaits scientific investigation.

and by the singing of the *Trisagion* ('Holy art thou O God,
Holy art thou O mighty, Holy art thou O immortal...') and
other hymns. The second is the 'Great Entrance' before the
eucharistic prayer, when the offerings of bread and wine are
carried in a more splendid procession, accompanied by
ministers bearing fans representing angels' wings and the
singing of the *Cherubikon* ('We who the cherubim do mystic-
ally show forth . . .')[1] The influence of the imperial court is
seen in the ceremonial in which the reverence paid to the
different orders of ministers, the sacred books, and eucharistic
elements is derived from the court etiquette of the time.

Inevitably the people's devotion tended to centre around
these processions which were all that they were permitted to see.
Moreover the Great Entrance is not an offertory procession
and therefore lacks direct association with the offering of the
Eucharist by the people. The setting apart of the elements
has already been performed behind the closed doors of the
ikonostasis by the celebrant and deacon in a preliminary service
called the *Prothesis*. This is the real offertory of the Eastern
liturgies. In the fully developed Byzantine form of this service
the crucifixion is symbolically re-enacted over the elements,
including the piercing of the bread with a 'spear'. This led
to the allegorical interpretation of the Great Entrance (see
especially Theodore of Mopsuestia) as the procession of the
crucified Christ to the tomb, though in recent times it has been
interpreted as representing the way of the cross. In either case
the consecration, which is regarded as taking place at the
Epiklesis, is related symbolically to the resurrection.

OTHER EASTERN LITURGIES

However, as we have already noted at the end of the last
chapter, some of the older Eastern liturgies, owing to the
historical circumstances of schism and to geographical remote-
ness from Byzantine influence, have survived and are in use

1 For the history of the interpretation of this procession see Dix,
The Shape of the Liturgy, pp. 282ff.

in the separated Churches to the present day. These are the Coptic and Ethiopian liturgies and the Syrian liturgies. None of them have entirely escaped the influence of the Byzantine liturgical development, but all of them retain some individual characteristics belonging to their own local tradition.

To give details of all the non-Byzantine liturgies available for study would be beyond the scope of this book. The Syrian liturgies have therefore been selected for special attention, partly because, being still in use in the Middle East and in India, they are of ecumenical importance for the development of worship in the younger churches of Asia; partly because their very distinctiveness and divergence from the Byzantine tradition gives them interest for the comparative study of liturgy. They are: (i) the *East Syrian Liturgy* attributed to the founders of the Church in Edessa, *St. Addai and St. Mari;* (ii) the *West Syrian Liturgy* of which the form most commonly used is the *Liturgy of St. James.*

THE LITURGY OF ST. ADDAI AND ST. MARI

This rite, whether in the earlier East Syrian form or in its Malabar variation,[1] is important for liturgical study as being composed in Syriac rather than in Greek. Other liturgies

[1] In the *Christian Topography* of Cosmas Indicopleustes, we learn that this East Syrian traveller visited India and Ceylon about A.D. 535 and found colonies of Christians, presumably foreign traders, settled on the west coast of India and in Ceylon. He reports that in the place called Kalliana (probably not Quilon, but a place on the mouth of the Bakanur river north of Calicut) there was a bishop appointed from Persia and that in Ceylon there were Persian Christians with a presbyter appointed from Persia 'and all the apparatus of public worship'. Although the history of the Indian Christians of St. Thomas before the sixteenth century is largely lost in obscurity, we may surmise that the Eucharists which Cosmas attended during his tour of this region were celebrated according to an East Syrian rite which differed little from the *Liturgy of St. Addai and St. Mari.* At any rate it is certain that it was a rite akin to Addai and Mari (often called the Malabar rite) which the Portuguese found in use in Kerala in the sixteenth century. Unlike *Addai and Mari,* it appears to have included the words of Institution before the Romans found it, but *outside* the eucharistic prayer,

geographically of Syrian origin—the *Liturgy of the Apostolic Constitutions,* the *Liturgy of St. James* and the *Liturgy of St. Chrysostom*—are Greek rather than Syrian in character. This is a matter of the style in which they are written as well as the theological concepts which they express. But the *Liturgy of St. Addai and St. Mari* was evidently transported to Edessa beyond the bounds of the Roman Empire before it became Hellenized. Connexions with the Greek Church were still further severed when the users of the rite seceded to form the Nestorian Church, in consequence of which it is sometimes referred to as the Nestorian or Chaldaean liturgy, though it was evidently composed before the time of Nestorius. Although there are marks of influence in a Byzantine direction, e.g., in the *Prothesis* (see above), the introduction of a Greek type of preface and the *Sanctus,* an intercession and *Anamnesis* which are different in style from the earliest stratum of the eucharistic prayer, it still remains the clearest example we have of a type of liturgy which may have been common among the Syriac-speaking people in the third and fourth centuries.

One remarkable feature is that the prayer appears to be addressed to Christ, though this has been obscured by the addition of an address to the Trinity at the beginning. Whether this address to Christ is primitive or whether it is due to emphasis on his divinity during the Arian controversy is uncertain.

A few quotations will show the character of this prayer.[1]

just before the fraction, which is a clear indication that the Words of Institution did not originally belong to this eucharistic prayer (see Dix, p. 179). Also the section from the lections to the Creed was different in order.

With some slight revision this rite is still in use by the Romo-Syrians, i.e., those Syrians who remained in communion with Rome, but continued in their traditional worship in Syriac. A group of Syrians who have joined the Church of Rome in recent years are permitted to use a revised form of the *Liturgy of St. James* (see below).

[1] Quoted from F. E. Brightman, *Liturgies Eastern and Western,* Vol. i, pp. 285ff.

After the commemoration of creation (leading to the Preface and *Sanctus* which have doubtless been added later) the prayer continues :

We give thanks to thee, O my God, even we thy servants weak and frail and miserable, for that thou hast given us great grace past recompense in that thou didst put on our manhood that thou mightest quicken it by thy godhead, and hast exalted our low estate and restored our fall and raised our mortality and forgiven our trespasses and justified our sinfulness and enlightened our knowledge and, O our Lord and our God, hast condemned our enemies and granted victory to the weakness of our frail nature in the overflowing mercies of thy grace.

After the interpolated intercession, the prayer goes on, probably originally in continuation of the above passage :

And we also, O my Lord, thy weak and frail and miserable servants, who are gathered together in thy Name, both stand before thee at this time and have received the example which is from thee delivered unto us.

This last clause is the only allusion in the prayer to the Last Supper. It is however pivotal to the whole prayer and takes the place of the Words of the Institution in other rites.[1] The *Epiklesis* which follows, is very different from the developed *Epiklesis* of the Greek liturgies from the fourth century onwards and is more like that of Hippolytus, i.e., not regarded as effecting consecration, but being essentially an invoking of Christ's presence and a prayer for the communicants :

And may there come, O my Lord, thine Holy Spirit and rest upon this offering of thy servants and bless it and

[1] We should not regard the Words of Institution as effecting consecration. As we have seen in our study of the earlier history of the Eucharist (p. 45) the essential structure of the liturgy is the repetition of our Lord's action of taking, blessing, breaking and giving. The Words of Institution are only the authority for this. At the same time, it was inevitable that these Words should be added if this rite was to continue in use.

hallow it that it be to us, O my Lord, for the pardon of offences and the remission of sins and for the great hope of resurrection from the dead and for new life in the kingdom of heaven with all those who have been well-pleasing in thy sight . . .

THE LITURGY OF ST. JAMES

This belongs to what is known as the *West Syrian* liturgical tradition. Close similarities between it and the rite referred to and quoted by Cyril of Jerusalem in his *Catechetical Sermons* reveal that it is basically the local rite of the see of Jerusalem which had possibly been revised in a Greek direction about the middle of the fourth century by Cyril himself. On the other hand there are differences between Cyril's rite and the *Liturgy of St. James* as we know it. Dix argues that the fourth-century rite of Jerusalem was adopted and revised in the early years of the fifth century by the patriarchal see of Antioch, and that this is the *Liturgy of St. James*.

While the patriarchal sees of Antioch and Jerusalem made *St. James* their norm, in NW. Syria a number of different *anaphoras* were used within the same general structure of the liturgy. Over seventy of these are extant and some of them are occasionally used by the Syrians of Kerala, some having primitive characteristics. This great variety indicates the continued assertion by the bishops of provincial dioceses in Syria of their ancient right to compose their own eucharistic prayers within a traditional pattern long after the great sees had standardized their rites. Even with regard to the normal rite Dix observes, 'Modern and medieval Monophysite MSS. of *St. James* differ textually from one another more considerably than those of any other rite—another symptom of the permanent lack of central authority in matters liturgical in Syria.'[1]

The Monophysite schism was a turning-point in the history

---

[1] *The Shape of the Liturgy*, p. 177.

F

of the *Liturgy of St. James*. When this occurred in the sixth century the rite had become the standard West Syrian tradition; but those who did not secede from the Greek Church soon abandoned it for the Byzantine rites, leaving its use to the schismatics. The latter used the Syriac revision, which underwent a series of further revisions during the Middle Ages, sometimes in a Byzantine direction (for the Syrians, though they were no longer in communion with Byzantium, could not rid themselves of respect for the Byzantine tradition as liturgically correct), sometimes revisions of an independent character. The Syriac version is now used only by a few congregations around Damascus, but it survives in Arabic and Malayalam translations.

Of the Greek version, which is no longer in use, little need be said.[1] Unlike the Syrian version, it has a Little Entrance and a Great Entrance which indicate Byzantine influence. The hymn which is sung at the Great Entrance is not the Byzantine *cherubikon*, but *Sigēsato pasa sarx broteia*, which has been magnificently paraphrased in the English hymn, 'Let all mortal flesh keep silence'. In it the words (more accurately translated than in the hymn), 'for the King of Kings, Christ our God now goes forth to be sacrificed and given as food to the faithful', would seem to imply that the Great Entrance in *St. James* is to be interpreted as representing the way of the cross rather than the procession to the tomb as in the Byzantine rite.[2] If this is earlier than the Byzantine tradition, the modern Orthodox reinterpretation of the Great Entrance noted above is a return to a more primitive typology.

THE LITURGY OF ST. JAMES IN INDIA

The variations in the *Liturgy of St. James* form a complex study. Those who wish to pursue it are referred to the notes

[1] For the text see Brightman, op. cit.

[2] Here we must differ from Dix who equates its meaning with that of the Byzantine Great Entrance.

in Brightman. It is sufficient to note that some of the later additions to the rite are among the more attractive features, e.g., the responses of the people during the *Anaphora*, 'Our Lord, thy death we commemorate . . .'[1] and 'Have mercy upon us, O God . . .' These responses closely associate the congregation with the celebrant and are part of the characteristic corporateness of the rite as celebrated by the Indian Syrians. Anyone who has attended the Syrian *Qurbana* (Eucharist) cannot have failed to be impressed by the full attendance of the congregation and the animated participation of the laity, led by the deacon, in the hymns and responses. We are probably nearer here to the spirit of the pre-Nicene Church than anywhere else in Christendom, even though the use of the rite in India belongs to a later period.[2]

There are no wooden or stone screens after the pattern of the Byzantine *ikonostasis* in Syrian churches. The nave is, however, separated from the choir by a rail or low wall and a curtain is drawn across the sanctuary during the long *Prothesis* at the beginning during which the people, led by the deacon, sing hymns. The curtain is withdrawn for the *Pre-anaphora* or liturgy of the catechumens and the *Anaphora* itself, so that the main part of the rite is visible and audible. It is drawn again for the Fraction and Commixture (placing of a piece of the consecrated bread in the chalice) and then withdrawn for the recitation of the Lord's Prayer and embolism (the

---

[1] This is a response also found in the Coptic rite and seems to have belonged to the Egyptian Liturgy at an early date and was presumably borrowed by the Syrians from the Copts. The second response is probably Byzantine in origin.

[2] The introduction of the *Liturgy of St. James* to India is not earlier than the latter part of the seventeenth century. Mar Gregorius, the first bishop to be sent by the Patriarch of Antioch after the revolt of the Syrians against the Roman Catholics, evidently celebrated according to this rite soon after his arrival in 1665, but was persuaded by his clergy to conform to the local rite of the East Syrian tradition as corrected by the Roman Catholics. The supersession of the latter by *St. James* was only gradual and may not have been complete until the nineteenth century. See L. W. Brown, op. cit.

prayer which takes up the last clause of thè Lord's Prayer and is said by the priest). This is followed by the elevation, which is marked by the ringing of bells (and the explosion of fireworks at festivals). The people join in a joyful colloquy with the deacon. After hymns of adoration the curtain is drawn again for the communion of the ministers, after which it is withdrawn for the priest to come down from the altar for the communion of the people. Unfortunately communion, for those who wish to receive it, now only takes place after the service is over, this displacement being in India of recent origin.

There are a few secret prayers said by the priest mostly during the litanies conducted by the deacon and following closely their content. The secret prayer which is most to be regretted is that of the first part of the eucharistic prayer said by the priest while the people sing the *Sanctus*. This means that the people pass abruptly from the *Sanctus* to the Words of Institution; but taken as a whole the rite has escaped the least satisfactory features of the post-Nicence liturgical development. The ceremonial provides an aura of splendour and mystery without preventing the full participation of the people in the whole movement of the liturgy.

The following is an outline of the service with some quotations[1]:

The Pre-anaphora

1. *Preparation and Prothesis.* After requesting the prayers of the people by silently stretching out his hands, the celebrant

---

[1] The quotations are mainly from *The Order of the Holy Qurbana of the Orthodox Syrian Church of Malabar*, translated by Mar Ivanios (S.P.C.K., printed C.M.S. Press, Kottayam). L. W. Brown, who gives a full account of the service in *The Indian Christians of St. Thomas*, pp. 213-232, regards this as the best recent translation and largely follows it in his own quotations. It does not, however, give the silent prayers which, where quoted, are from Dr. Brown's translation. The author is indebted in this account to Dr. Brown and to the chapter on the Holy Qurbana in *Ways of Worship* (C.L.S.—*not* the S.C.M. publication of the same title).

with other ministers puts on his vestments and prepares the elements behind the drawn curtain, reciting set prayers.

2. *The Lections:* Priest : Mary that brought thee forth and John that baptized thee shall intercede for us. Have mercy upon us.

The people respond to this with a prayer to Christ glorifying him for his incarnation, death and resurrection.

Censing of the people.

The *Trisagion* ('Holy art thou O God . . .').

Kyrie eleison ('Lord have mercy') three times.

The Epistle, in a setting of hymns, biddings by the deacon, and responses.

The Gospel with candles, incense and ceremony, corresponding to the Little Entrance of the Byzantine liturgies.

(The lections vary on Sundays, festivals and special occasions. On other days they are Ephesians 4. 1-7 and Mark 3. 31-35. The deacon has read the Old Testament lection from the lectionary during the earlier preparations).

Deacon : *Stoumen Kalōs* (Let us stand well).

Congregation : *Kyrie eleison* (Lord have mercy).

3. *The Prayers. Proemion* (Preface).

Prayer for Absolution (Private confession has been made before the service by those who intend to receive communion.)

Sedra (Syriac : 'a set form of prayer')

There are many alternative pairs of *proemion* and *sedra,* but the prayer for absolution does not vary. The following is a quotation from one of the *sedra:*

. . . at this awful and terrible moment . . . the angels tremble, the archangels are afraid, the principalities wonder, the powers sing thee Halleluiah, the cherubim bless thee, the seraphim with their quick and incorporeal and flaming eyes look, and, beholding the Holy Spirit descend quickly and invisibly and hover and abide upon these offerings and sanctify them, sing 'Holy, Holy, Holy . . .'.

4. *The Nicene Creed.* This is preceded by a blessing of the censer in the name of the Trinity and accompanied by a censing of the people, which implies that only those who believe in the Trinity should remain.

The Anaphora

1. *The Kiss of Peace.* The celebrant kisses the chains of the censer. The deacon kisses the hand of the celebrant and the chains and then passes the greeting to one of the laity in the form of a handclasp and they pass it from one to another in the same way. This form of the greeting is peculiar to the Syrian Churches.[1] In the Roman Catholic and Orthodox Churches the Kiss is now exchanged only among the clergy ministering and no longer given to the people. Before giving the kiss the celebrant prays: '... that purified from all guile and all hypocrisy, we may greet one another with a kiss holy and divine ...'

2. *Prayer for the acceptance of the sacrifice,* similar in content to the Anglican Prayer of Humble Access. This is preceded by a colloquy between the deacon and the people and a brief prayer of blessing said by the priest.

3. A blessing adapted from 2 Cor. 13. 14, followed by an expanded *Sursum corda,* etc.

4. *Preface, Sanctus, Benedictus* ('Blessed is he that *hath come and is to come* in the Name of the Lord God : Hosanna in the highest').

5. *Commemoration of the Creation, Fall and Redemption,* said silently by the priest during the Sanctus. At the beginning of it he waves his hands over the elements to signify the descent of the Holy Spirit. The prayer, which takes up the words of the Sanctus, is :

[1] A simplified form of it has been adopted by the Church of South India.

Holy art thou, King of the ages and giver of all holiness, holy is thy Son, Jesus Christ our Lord, holy also is thy Holy Spirit, who searches all things, even the deep things of thee. Thou madest man out of dust and bestowedst upon him the delight of paradise; and when he transgressed thy command and fell, thou didst not despise nor forsake him, but didst call him by thy law, and instruct him by the prophets; and in the fulness of time thou didst send into the world thy only-begotten Son, who being incarnate of the Holy Spirit and the Virgin Mary renewed thy image in mankind.

6. *The Words of Institution*, freely adapted from the New Testament accounts,[1] and accompanied by the blessing and breaking of the bread (without as yet separating its parts) and the blessing of the chalice.

7. *Anamnesis* (memorial of the Passion and Resurrection) and *Oblation* (of 'this bloodless sacrifice'). This is preceded and concluded by two responses of the people. The former takes up the expanded version of the Words of Institution and introduces the *Anamnesis*. The latter is a phrase from the *Gloria in excelsis* (Glory to God in the highest).

8. *Epiklesis* (Invocation of the Holy Spirit).

The priest again waves his hands.

The deacon says : *Barekmore*.[2]

My beloved, how fearful is this moment and how dreadful is this time when the Holy Spirit descends from heaven,

---

1 This free adaptation and expansion of the Words of Institution is found in varying forms in all the ancient liturgies. It is a reminder of the time when the local eucharistic traditions were independent of the written books of the New Testament.

2 This means, 'Bless, Sir' (i.e., the priest) or possibly, 'Bless, Lord' (i.e., God). This is an oft-repeated petition by the deacon to the priest before he turns to the people to lead their devotions. The meaning is that the link between the people and the eucharistic action which is being performed at the altar is repeatedly renewed by a blessing from the altar and the deacon's function, as in all eastern liturgies, is to be the agent in maintaining that link.

from the heights above, and dwells upon this Holy Qurbana, and sanctifies it. Stand ye in silence and pray.

People : May peace be with us all and goodwill to us all.

Meanwhile the priest has been saying a silent prayer, after which he says aloud three times, 'Give answer to me, O Lord', and the people respond with a threefold *Kyrie eleison.*

The priest then waves his right hand over the paten and chalice in turn and makes a threefold sign of the cross over each, praying that the Holy Spirit may 'abide and transmute this bread into ... the very Body of our God, the Messiah', and 'perfect the chalice into ... the very Blood of our God, the Messiah'.

The people respond, 'Amen', and the *Epiklesis* continues in prayer for the communicants and the Church. It is clear that, as in the Greek liturgies, the *Epiklesis* is regarded as the moment of consecration.

9. *The Great Intercession.* This is a lengthy devotion of six sections in each of which the deacon, after saying *'Barekmore',* leads the people with a bidding prayer to which they respond, *'Kyrie eleison'.* The priest, who has offered a silent prayer during the bidding, says an intercession aloud and the people respond 'Amen'.

The intercession includes the reading of the *diptychs* in which are contained the names of the departed. This is a feature of all liturgies after the fifth century.

10. *The Fraction and Commixture.* An elaborate ceremony performed behind the drawn curtain.

Meanwhile the people sing the Seraphic Hymn based on the vision of the prophet of Isaiah 6.[1]

11. *The Catholic.* A devotion preparatory to communion which includes further commemoration of the saints and the

---

[1] Do not confuse this, as does *Ways of Worship* (C.L.S.), with the *Cherubikon* (cherubic hymn) of the Byzantine liturgies and its parallel, 'Let all mortal flesh keep silence', in the Greek *Liturgy of St. James.*

departed and the Lord's Prayer with protocol (prayer introductory to it) and embolism (prayer which expands its final
clause).

12. *The Elevation.* The priest lifts up the paten and the
chalice and this act is accompanied by a variation of the
ancient Eastern *hagia hagiois* ('Holy things for holy people': see
p. 63) and responses.

This is followed by a brief bidding : 'Let us remember at
Qurbanas and prayers our fathers who while on earth taught
us to be the children of God.'

13. *The Eucharistic Adoration* includes metrical hymns in
praise of the Virgin Mary and the saints each of which ends
with *'Barekmore'* and the Gloria.

At the close the celebrant again asks silently for the prayers
of the people. There may be a sermon at this point, if it has
not been preached after the Gospel.

14. *The Procession of the Holy Mysteries.* After the priest
has received communion himself and administered it to those
in the sanctuary, he comes down the sanctuary steps bearing
the chalice and paten, accompanied by candles on either side
and a thurifer before him. The act is marked by the ringing
of bells, praises and responses. This is the proper time for the
people to receive communion; but now they receive it after
the service.

15. *The Post-communion prayers and Blessing.* These are
followed by a post-communion service which the priest performs in private behind the closed curtain. After an interval
the people say the *Kauma* (Trisagion), certain brief prayers,
the Lord's Prayer and the Hail Mary. They then pray aloud
their own prayers, so that there is a noise like 'the voice of
many waters', after which those not receiving communion
depart and those who are to receive remain and do so half
privately by intinction (i.e., both elements together, the bread
moistened by the wine).

THE *QURBANA* IN THE MAR THOMA CHURCH

The Mar Thoma Church, which is a branch of the Syrian Church reformed under Anglican influence during the nineteenth century, has a liturgy compiled by its chief reformer, Abraham Malpan. His aim was to express change of doctrine with as little change as possible in the liturgical form. There is no prayer to (or through) the saints and most of the references to the saints are omitted. The dead are remembered but not prayed for. The Holy Spirit is invoked to 'sanctify this bread' instead of to 'abide and transmute' it. The curtain is not closed at the Fraction and ministers' communion. In the communion of the people the bread and wine are given separately, a spoon being used to administer the wine.[1]

While the Western liturgical tradition has not been without its influence on the Syrian tradition in India, particularly in the case of the Romo-Syrians and also the Mar Thoma Church, which came under Anglican influence, there has been a reciprocal influence of Syrian forms on the Churches born of Protestant missions in India, as we shall see when we come to observe recent liturgical developments in the Lutheran Churches in India, the Anglican Communion in India, Pakistan, Burma and Ceylon, and the Church of South India.

[1] For these and other details see *Ways of Worship* (C.L.S.), pp. 48f. The Mar Thoma Church also publishes in Kottayam English translations of its services.

CHAPTER 6

THE LITURGIES OF THE WEST

WE have already studied the descriptions of the Eucharist
in Rome in the second and early third centuries as given by
Justin and Hippolytus. At this time Greek was still the
liturgical language in the capital city. There is insufficient
evidence for us to give an exact date for the change from
Greek to Latin as the liturgical language in Rome; but this
had probably begun to take place by the middle of the third
century, when Latin begins to appear in the inscriptions on
the tombs of Popes. There is evidence, however, in a Greek
quotation from a eucharistic prayer by a Roman orator in the
year 360 that even then Greek had not entirely gone out of
use in Roman worship. In Africa, though Tertullian gives
some liturgical quotations in Greek, Latin was in use in the
time of Cyprian. All extant liturgical texts of the West, other
than that of Hippolytus, are in Latin, which, as the language
of Western culture, continued in use throughout the Middle
Ages and is still the language of Roman liturgical worship
today; though the Missal and other liturgical books have been
translated into many languages and experiments have been
inaugurated in vernacular worship.

The liturgical traditions of the West may be divided into
three groups, the Roman, the Gallican, the North African.
For convenience of exposition we shall treat these in the
reverse order, as it was the Roman rite which finally prevailed
throughout western Christendom with some modifications of
Gallican origin.

1. NORTH AFRICA

No liturgical text survives from this area, and we can only make conjectures from references to the Eucharist in Tertullian, Cyprian and Augustine and some decrees of North African councils.

It is evident from these references that the history of liturgical development followed much the same pattern in the early centuries as elsewhere, i.e., a fluid rite with certain local characteristics, but with the general structure common to all Christendom. There were borrowings from the liturgies of both East and West, e.g., Augustine's church at Hippo had probably not adopted the *Epiklesis,* while some other churches had. As in Rome, the kiss of peace precedes Communion instead of coming before the *Anaphora,* as in the East. There are also signs in Cyprian of a doctrine of the eucharistic sacrifice tending towards the later developed Roman doctrine.

Church Councils at the end of the fourth century were evidently concerned to restrict uncontrolled variety and borrowing by celebrants. Canon 23 of the Third Council of Carthage (397) enacts that all prayers at the altar are to be directed to the Father, and that 'whatever prayers anyone had written for himself or derived from other sources should not be used by him till he had referred them to his more learned brethren'. Similarly the First Council of Milevis (402) enacts that only such prayers should be used by all as had been approved in synod.[1] These are examples of the trend of liturgical development which prevailed throughout the Church.

2. THE GALLICAN RITES

Of the four local subdivisions of this liturgical tradition we may for our purpose ignore the *Milanese* and the *Celtic.* Though Milan may possibly have had an important part to play in the original dissemination of these rites, the church

[1] Quoted from Srawley, *The Early History of the Liturgy,* p. 146.

there adopted the Roman *Canon* (consecration prayer) before or during the episcopate of Ambrose (end of fourth century). Milan is still permitted by the Church of Rome to celebrate according to its own rite; but the relics of a non-Roman tradition are fragmentary. The *Celtic Rite* (e.g., as found in the Stowe and Bobbio Missals) is a mixed rite such as one might expect itinerant Celtic missionaries to compile from the liturgies they encountered in their travels, and therefore not a pure development of a local liturgical tradition. It soon retreated before the advance of Anglo-Saxon Christianity and was superseded in England after the Synod of Whitby by the Roman rite.

The two characteristic variations of this tradition, which are so similar in structure that we may presume a common origin, are : (1) The *Mozarabic* or *Old Spanish* liturgy which is still in use in a chapel of the cathedral of Toledo where Cardinal Ximenes arranged for its perpetuation about 1500. The manuscripts of it then available showed traces of Roman influence. But by using manuscripts discovered at the end of the nineteenth century it has been possible to establish a pure form of the rite as it was current before the Moorish invasion (711). (2) The *Gallican* Liturgy was the order in France and Germany during the earlier part of the Middle Ages. Although it ceased to be used in the eighth century, we have documentary evidence of it in the so-called *Missale Gothicum,* probably from Alsace, the lectionary of Luxeuil (seventh century) the Reichenau fragments, references in the writings of Gregory of Tours (sixth century) and the *Expositio Missae* (seventh century), to mention the most important sources.

The most obvious difference between the liturgies of East and West is in the matter of variable prayers. In the East there is a variation of lections and liturgical hymns according to the Church's year. In the Byzantine tradition some variability is provided by the occasional use of the *Liturgy of St. Basil* instead of the normal *St. Chrysostom,* and there are similar possibilities in the Coptic tradition. In the Syrian tradition, as we have seen, there is a choice of *proemions* and *sedras* and a wide choice of *anaphoras* which may occasionally be substituted for the normal *anaphora* of *St. James*. But in all this there is nothing to compare with the psalms, lections and prayers in various parts of the Roman Mass which vary regularly according to the Calendar. In the Gallican rites this variation is carried to a unique degree. Whereas in Rome the *Canon* remained fixed, in the Gallican tradition not only certain prayers, but the whole series, became subject to variation, including the eucharistic 'proper', which was not a single continuous prayer but a sequence of separate prayers. There were, indeed, ordinary Mass formulas, such as those of the Reichenau fragments, which could be used when no special order was provided; but for the festivals of our Lord and most saints' days there was provided in effect a special liturgy for that day alone.

The order is as follows :

1. *Fourfold song sequence.*
    a. Psalm (= Roman *introit,* i.e., entrance of the clergy).
    b. After the celebrant has greeted the congregation, 'The Lord be with you alway', the *Trisagion* is sung in Greek and Latin.
    c. *Kyrie eleison* sung by three boys.
    d. *Benedictus* (Hymn of Zachariah).

2. *Collect and Lections.*
    a. Lection from the Old Testament, followed by *Benedictus es* (part of the song of Shadrach, Meshach and Abednego).
    b. The Epistle, followed by the *Trisagion* again.
    c. The Gospel, with a solemn procession similar to the Little Entrance of the Byzantine liturgies, again followed by the *Trisagion*.

3. *Sermon.*

4. *Intercession for the Church.*
   a. for the faithful.
   b. for the catechumens, who are then dismissed.
   Both parts are introduced by the deacon's litany as in the East.

5. The beginning of the Mass proper—*The Offertory Procession* accompanied by hymns.

6. An address, called *praefatio missae* or *missa,* expounds the meaning of the feast of the day and is followed by a prayer.

7. *Kiss of Peace* followed by prayer.

8. *The Eucharistic Prayers.*
   a. 'The Lord be with you,' 'Lift up your hearts,' etc.
   b. Preface—called *immolatio* or *contestatio.*
   c. *Sanctus.*
   d. *Post Sanctus.* A prayer of transition from the *Sanctus* to the Words of Institution.
   e. The Words of Institution.
   f. *Anamnesis* and *Epiklesis,* together called *post secreta* or *post mysterium.*

9. *The Communion.*
   a. Fraction with complex ceremonial and accompanied by antiphonal chant.
   b. Lord's Prayer with protocol and embolism.
   c. If a bishop is celebrating, the deacon invites the people to receive his blessing which is then given.
   d. Communion accompanied by the chanting of Psalm 33 or some other song.
   e. Post-communion prayer and dismissal.

As an illustration of the character of Gallican prayers and

the contrast between them and those of the more austere Roman tradition the following translation is given of the Mozarabic and Roman collects for Epiphany :

Mozarabic. O king of all the ages, Christ, the most high God, who in the days of Herod the king wast born of a virgin and declared by a new star to the wise men who sought thee; may the protection of thy power be revealed in us to drive away all the rulers of darkness; and may the star of thy majesty so shine in us that no obstacles of error may prevent our seeking thee. May we run to see thee and rejoice straightway in the vision of thee.

Roman. O God who on this day didst reveal thine only begotten Son to the nations by the leading of a star; mercifully grant that we who know thee now by faith may be led to contemplate the vision of thy glory; through the same Lord Jesus Christ . . .

THE ORIGIN OF THE GALLICAN RITES

These rites are only known to us from manuscripts dating from the sixth century. Opinion is divided as to when this liturgical type had its origin. Duchesne, a liturgist of the end of the nineteenth century, conjectured that it came to the West from the East through Milan in the fourth century. Milan was then the residence of the Emperors and had at least one Greek bishop, Auxentius (355-74). This conjecture has for some time been unpopular among liturgists, who have favoured the theory of a local development of the fluid rite of the West with some few borrowings from the East; but it is interesting to find that Jungmann is inclined to favour it as accounting (*a*) for the many similarities of Gallican to Eastern usage, (*b*) for the developed character of these rites, which demand a date not earlier than the fourth century for such development, (*c*) for the probability that such a widespread tradition emanated from some authoritative centre. The influence of Milan is known to have extended as far as Spain.

It is no objection that, if Milan was the mediator of this type of liturgy, it is difficult to account for the fact that the Church there abandoned it before the end of the fourth century. In this period of transition this might easily have occurred under the influence of an Italian bishop such as Ambrose. There is the greater difficulty that the Gallican tradition is at least as near to the Roman tradition as to the Eastern. If we accept Duchesne's conjecture provisionally, we must also presume that the eastern liturgical text or texts which came to Spain and Gaul were introduced into a vigorous local way of worship which radically influenced the development therefrom, particularly in the matter of variable prayers, and that the many special liturgies for festivals were local compositions within the given structure of the archetype.

The Gallican prayers tended to be excessively verbose, faulty in their construction, so that one is not always certain whether the Father or the Son is being addressed, and provincial in their Latin style. They were the homespun liturgies of the dark ages, which could only satisfy the peoples of north-west Europe during their emergence from barbarism. It is not surprising that with the advance of culture in the Carolingian empire of the eighth century there should have been a growing preference for the better constructed and more polished Mass of Rome. Many may deplore the eventual disappearance of Gallican freedom and variety, but we must also reflect that most of the medieval developments in the Mass which are now deplored by Roman liturgists as well as non-Roman were due to the impact of Gallican influence on the Roman rite in the country of its adoption.

3. ROME: THE EARLIEST EVIDENCE

As with the Gallican rites, the origins of the order for the Mass in the city of Rome are one of the unsolved puzzles of liturgical study. Between the compactly constructed Greek Canon of Hippolytus at the beginning of the third century

G

and the first evidence of the Latin Canon[1] with its complex gradations there is a gap of more than a century and a half.

One possible source of liturgical material adopted by the Roman Church is that of the eucharistic tradition of Egypt. Several similarities of wording have been noted between the Mass and the Egyptian *Liturgy of St. Mark*. In particular there is the petition that the eucharistic sacrifice should be taken by the ministry of an angel to the heavenly altar and that God should accept it as he did the sacrifices of Abel and Abraham. These petitions occur in the intercessory prayers before the *Anaphora* in the *Liturgy of St. Mark*, whereas they come after the Words of Institution in the Canon of the Mass. We know that there was much intercourse between Rome and Alexandria, as Rome received her corn supply from there. Also the great Athanasius, Bishop of Alexandria, was welcomed in Rome by Pope Julius during one of his flights into exile. We do not know whether this was an occasion for liturgical borrowing, nor can we say that the borrowing was necessarily all on one side. Athanasius or other Alexandrian visitors might well have taken back with them phrases borrowed from the eucharistic prayer or prayers in use in Rome at the time and incorporated them into their own liturgy.

The most important evidence from the end of the fourth century is contained in *De Sacramentis*, the instructions given to the newly-baptized by Ambrose, Bishop of Milan. He quotes a large part of the Canon in almost exactly the same words as those found in all later texts of it, and some of the

[1] The word 'Canon' is an abbreviation of *canon actionis* = the order of eucharistic action. It is equivalent to the Greek *Anaphora*. In the early centuries the Roman Canon was regarded as commencing with the Preface and concluding with the Doxology and 'Amen' at the end of the eucharistic prayer. But since the eighth century the Preface came to be regarded as separate from the Canon and the latter as only beginning *after* the *Sanctus*. On the other hand the Canon is now regarded as including the Lord's Prayer, the *Agnus Dei* (O Lamb of God) and even the Communion.

differences which appear may be due to his quoting from memory. The Canon when it was first composed was probably one of the many experimental eucharistic prayers which happened to gain the authoritative acceptance of the Church. But from that time it has hardly changed at all, the only additions being some intercessory passages not found in Ambrose. From another reference in his *De Sacramentis* it seems probable that in his time the intercessions 'for the people, for kings and for others' came before the Canon in their more primitive position. Indeed this general prayer for the Church, divided into a prayer for the catechumens and a prayer for the faithful, is still mentioned as in use in a letter of Pope Felix (483-92) a century later.

Up to this time the Roman Mass was no doubt already adorned with some splendour of ceremonial and singing, though as yet without instruments; but it must have been in essence a severely simple rite, powerfully direct in its concentration on the eucharistic action and giving expression to the Roman genius for brevity. It started immediately with the lections and sermon, proceeded to the prayer for the Church and then, after the dismissal of the catechumens, went on to the offertory, salutation, *Sursum corda,* etc., Preface, Proper Preface, *Sanctus,* Canon,[1] with the Kiss of Peace, Fraction and Lord's Prayer[2] followed by Communion and then, possibly with

---

[1] As in Ambrose's account, but with the addition of prayers for the offerers, as mentioned in the letter of Pope Innocent I to Bishop Decentius of Gubbio in the year 416. This was parallel to the Eastern reading of the diptychs (prayers for the living and the dead) and was the beginning of the inclusion of intercessions in the Canon.

[2] Note the original position of the Lord's Prayer *after* the Fraction. It is there intended as a prayer of preparation for Communion. Gregory the Great transferred it to a position immediately after the Canon, as in the Byzantine rites, so that it is now regarded as attached to the Canon rather than to Communion. Gregory evidently regarded it as most suitable that 'we should say our Redeemer's own prayer over his body and blood', i.e., before the former has been taken from the altar and handed to the presbyters for the Fraction.

a brief post-communion prayer, the deacon's dismissal of the people :

Ite, missa est: 'Go, it is the dismissal.'[1]

ROMAN LITURGICAL BOOKS

For the history of the Mass so far our evidence has been references to the rite in treatises and letters. Before we pass on to the Mass as it found its permanent shape in the centuries following the fourth, we must note the character of the liturgical texts from which our knowledge is derived.

In the Churches of the Reformation which came into being after the invention of printing we are familiar with service books containing all the material for any form of worship and possessed by ministers and laymen alike. In the early centuries, however, different books were written for the different persons or groups taking part in the services, giving their prescribed words and actions. One is reminded of a sacred drama in which each actor is given his part in manuscript to learn. This very character of the older liturgical books is a striking illustration of the corporateness and co-operative spirit of ancient worship.

For the celebrant at the Mass and other sacraments, whether bishop or priest, there was the *sacramentary* containing the variable passages which he had to read. The 'ordinary' or fixed part including the Canon, is not found in the earlier sacramentaries. The celebrant would know these by heart, or he might read the canon from a separate tablet.

---

[1] This was the formula for the end of a trial in Court or the end of an audience with an important person. The word *missa* (= dismissal), first used for the formal ending of any service and then of any service which contained such a formal dismissal, came to be restricted to the Eucharist. Hence the Roman word *Missa* = Mass. Some who use the word defend it on the ground that, being of little meaning in itself, it can be given the content of the Church's eucharistic theology. A better interpretation is that it lays emphasis on the gathering of the people of God before they are sent forth after receiving sacramental grace to their work and witness in the world.

There were two different books of lections, one for the reader of the Epistle called the *apostolus,* the other for the deacon who read the Gospel called the *evangelium* or gospel book. There were books for the singers, such as the *antiphonal,* and the *cantatorium* for the individual singer who led the chants between the lections. The *ordines* or rubric books contained the directions for the minister who directed the movement of the celebration. These books were particularly necessary for festivals when the variations in ritual and cere-monial were more complex. Hence we learn most about the festal services from them.

Only later, from the thirteenth century onwards, the sacra-mentary was displaced by the *missale plenum* or *missal* which contained everything necessary for the Mass, while everything required for the recitation of the Daily Office (see p. 151) was brought together in the *breviary,* and everything required for Baptism and other sacraments in the *ritual.* This new form of service book was of great convenience to itinerant clergy, such as the Franciscans. It was also necessary for the growing practice of the priest's celebration without the assistance of the ministers.

To return to the sacramentary, there are three sacrament-aries from which we have knowledge of the old Roman form of the Mass. These were named in the last century after the three popes with whom they were thought to be connected. They are collections of the variable prayers (collects, secrets—offertory prayers—prefaces and post-communion prayers) to be used by the popes when they 'held stations', i.e., celebrated on different Sundays at different churches in Rome.

1. *The Leonine Sacramentary.* This was completed in the sixth century, the extant manuscripts of it belonging to the seventh. Its connexion with Pope Leo is uncertain. It appears to be a private collection of various mass formulas and is particularly rich in its collection of proper prefaces, 267 in number; whereas in the later *Gregorian Sacramentary* there are only fourteen.

2. *The Gelasian Sacramentary* is only found entire in an eighth-century MS. from Gaul into which some Gallican elements have intruded. The core of this may well go back to Pope Gelasius (see below). There are also several MSS. of a mixed sacramentary composed of Gelasian, other Roman, and Gallican elements, known as the *Frankish Gelasian;* but this is evidence for the period of transition when Roman traditions began to be introduced into Gaul and prepared the way for the final synthesis at the end of the eighth century.

3. *The Gregorian Sacramentary.* The MSS. of this are late and of Frankish origin; but by critical methods it has been possible to discover earlier forms of it. We shall see later the importance of this sacramentary in the history of the Mass. In all probability it was originally produced by Pope Gregory the Great himself.

THE REVISED ROMAN RITE

About the time of Pope Gelasius I (492-6) some radical changes were made in the Mass. Firstly the great intercession for the Church disappears. The only relic of it in its original position is the celebrant's 'Let us pray'; and then silence, followed by the offertory. By this time the catechumens were no longer excluded from the 'Mass of the Faithful', and it doubtless seemed unnecessary to have an intercession intended in its first part to precede their dismissal, which then did not take place.

The intercession, however, was far from being lost altogether. It may be compared to a bursting seed pod scattering in different directions its contents which took root and developed in different parts of the service. First, and probably before its final disappearance, intercessory passages were introduced into the Canon. These may have been another reason for regarding the original intercession as superfluous. It is also probable that the offertory prayers (*secreta*), now said silently, were an adaptation to a new purpose of the collects said by the priest during the general intercession.[1] Another intercessory act, which may be the old intercession itself, now displaced, is the processional litany which on certain occasions is chanted before the beginning of Mass.[2] A vestigial remain of the old intercession is also found in the *Kyrie eleison* at the beginning of the fore-Mass itself, originally, as in the Eastern liturgies, repeated three times, but expanded in Rome as the nine-fold *Kyrie* (*Kyrie eleison* said three times, *Christe eleison* three times, and again *Kyrie eleison* three times). This phrase is, of course, the traditional response in the Greek liturgy. But the petitions of the Litany, chanted by the deacon, have disappeared : only these responses and the prayer with which they concluded, namely, the Collect,[3] remain, and these have been divided one from the other by the later insertion of the ministers' preparation (psalms, antiphon, confessions, versicles and responses and prayers) said at the foot of the altar steps, and the *Gloria in excelsis* on the days for which it is appointed.

Also before the *Kyrie* is the *introit* (entrance psalm), and the whole sequence forms an impressive introduction to the lections with which the service began until well on into the fifth century.[4] It is parallel, though different in content, to the *Enarxis* (beginning) of the Byzantine liturgies. This introductory part of the service was built up because of the necessity of providing a dignified entrance for the ministers in the great basilicas. In fact, as we have already noted in the case of the

1 It was these offertory prayers which possibly provided Cranmer with the basis for the great intercession in the Anglican order for Holy Communion; or he may have taken as his model the bidding prayers of *Prone* (see below) which appear to have been introduced into England from France not later than the beginning of the fifteenth century, and possibly at the Norman conquest.

2 This was the exemplar for the Litany in the Anglican *Book of Common Prayer*.

3 *Collecta* means the gathering together by the celebrant of the preceding petitions of the people.

4 An interesting comfirmation that the service began with the lections comes from Augustine, *The City of God* (22. 8). Even on Easter Day 426 he began the Eucharist with the greeting ('The Lord be with you') and then the lections. See Jungmann, op. cit., i, p. 262.

Eastern rites, all the early liturgical texts which have survived were composed for celebration by bishops in the grand manner. This is particularly true of the *Gregorian Sacramentary* which was to be the basis for the Mass of the Middle Ages (see below). It is a papal Mass book containing orders for feast days and 'stational' Masses, i.e., Masses celebrated by the Pope on different Sundays in the different basilicas of Rome. Eventually the ordinary priest's Mass had to conform to this pattern, which was not really suited to parochial worship.

One survival of the ancient order in the modern Roman missal must be mentioned. In the Mass appointed for Good Friday[1] the service begins with the collect only and lections, and the old intercessory prayers are found in their original place and form. Bidding prayers are given (now by the priest, but originally probably by the deacon) for the Church, the Pope, the clergy and the faithful, rulers, catechumens, all men according to their needs, heretics and schismatics, the conversion of the Jews, the conversion of the pagans. After each bidding the deacon bids the people kneel for silent prayer and then rise for the collect said by the priest.[2]

---

[1] There is no consecration on Good Friday. The communion of the people, however, which had lapsed since the Council of Trent has been restored since 1955 and is given from the reserved sacrament. This had the rather curious name, the Mass of the pre-sanctified (*missa praesanctificatorum*), meaning that the elements have been consecrated on a previous day; but the name has been discontinued since 1955, as the service is now one of communion only and no longer resembles a Mass.

[2] The three Anglican collects for Good Friday are distilled from this great intercession. This and many other features in the Holy Week liturgy are signal illustrations of what has sometimes been called 'Baumstark's liturgical law', because he was the liturgist who first defined it: 'The preservation of that which is ancient in a season liturgically of high value.' This is not, of course, a legal or canonical law but a scientific one based upon observation of what actually has happened in the history of the liturgy. It is as much psychological as liturgical. We see it operating in our own parishes, where our people demand the old traditional hymns, for instance, at Christmas and would protest vigorously against a bright young minister with a knowledge of hymnody who tried to make them sing only new

In the Middle Ages a new form of intercession developed in certain localities. In France this was called the prayers for *Prone*[1]—a little service following the sermon at Mass with biddings in the vernacular. In Germany from the sixteenth century onwards a general vernacular prayer was said by the whole congregation. These excellent acts of intercession still survive in some parts of France and Germany.

DEVELOPMENTS IN CEREMONIAL

In the sixth and seventh centuries there was a great development of ceremonial at Rome, as we learn from *Ordo Romanus I* of the seventh century, one of the early rubric books, which gives the directions for the Pope's 'stational' celebration of the Mass. He arrives at the basilica at which he is to celebrate with a great retinue and there is vested with alb, scarf, tunicle, dalmatic, chasuble and pallium. When the great company of bishops, presbyters, deacons, sub-deacons and acolytes are ready in their appropriate vestments, the Pope gives a signal for the procession to start by picking up his maniple (originally a hand towel, now a small vestment worn on the wrist) perhaps in imitation of the Roman magistrates who started the games by throwing down a hand towel. The introit at once begins and the procession moves forward into church, the Pope preceded by incense and seven torches held by acolytes and supported by two deacons on either side. All these signs of honour are those to which the emperor and higher officers of state were entitled.

Although, however, there are some flourishes of ceremony

and better ones. They may tolerate or even welcome a revised liturgy on a Sunday after Trinity; but woe betide the presbyter who tries to introduce it on Easter Day. Even our liturgy committees engaged in prayer book revision will be careful to retain the old collects and lections for the great feasts and fasts, whatever they change in those prescribed for other days. It is a recognition of this law which enables liturgists in their researches to trace some of the more ancient elements in the later form of liturgies.

[1] French for *praeconium* = announcement.

during the service, e.g., the kissing of the Pope's foot by the deacon before reading the Gospel and much kissing of the Gospel-book afterwards, the main action of the rite still retains its essential simplicity and corporate character. The people, though they now leave the singing of hymns and responses to the choir, bring up their gifts of bread and wine at the offertory, the Pope himself receiving the first of these from the nobility. Some of the offerings are used in the celebration. The Canon is said in an audible voice facing the people with the various orders of ministers grouped around, and the only ceremonial action in it is the elevation at the end in which the archdeacon assists by elevating the chalice while the Pope elevates the bread.

The bishops and presbyters present perform the fraction after the Pope has broken the first bread. After receiving the bread the Pope mingles a fragment of it with the consecrated chalice before receiving the wine. In the communion of the clergy and people the Pope and the archdeacon begin the distribution and others carry on. Chalices are filled with wine which is consecrated by the addition of a few drops of wine from the one chalice which the Pope has consecrated.[1]

THE BLENDING OF ROMAN AND GALLICAN

We have already noted the growing preference in the Frankish empire of the eighth century for the Roman rather than the Gallican tradition, and various transitional combinations of the two. This culminated in the request of Charlemagne to Pope Hadrian I for an authoritative text of the Roman rite so that he might issue a uniform text within his empire. Hadrian sent him about A.D. 785 a copy of the *Gregorian Sacramentary* as then in use. This, however, only contained the liturgies prescribed for the more important holy days. The English scholar Alcuin, who had migrated to France, was entrusted with the task of editing it. This he did

[1] See Jungmann, i, pp. 66-74.

by adding a supplement containing what was required for parochial services and bringing together both Roman and Gallican traditions. As time went on, much of the material of the supplement as well as of the Gelasian Sacramentary was transferred to Alcuins' edition of the Gregorian Sacramentary with the result that a new type of Mass liturgy emerged—the Romano-Frankish.

After this had spread with a number of variations through France and Germany, it only remained for it to displace the old Roman liturgy in Italy and Rome itself. This occurred in the tenth and eleventh centuries when the cultural and political standing of Rome had declined and that of Germany predominated. New manuscripts were being produced in the scriptoria of Germany rather than of Italy, and the mass-books which thus came southwards were of the new type. Even the German emperors sometimes intervened in liturgical matters. When Henry II came to Rome in 1014 for his imperial coronation, he asked that the Creed might be sung at Mass as it was in his own country. This new development did not, however, mean complete uniformity. Much variety of practice continued until the end of the Middle Ages.

THE LATER DEVELOPMENT OF THE MASS

Though the intention of Alcuin and those who accepted his revision was doubtless to be true to the Roman tradition which they had adopted, subtle changes soon came over the eucharistic celebration. Some of these were no doubt due to the different temperament of the northern peoples of Europe, others to the changing concept of the Church as a hierarchy of clergy and laity rather than the mystical Body of the redeemed in Christ, and of the Eucharist as the means of guaranteeing Christ's presence rather than as the offering of the People of God.

There was first of all a heightening of the sensuousness and dramatic aspect of the celebration. This was seen in the increased use of the censer, the elaboration of ceremonial at the reading of the Gospel, the elevation of the elements at the consecration, accompanied by the ringing of the bells, that the people might at least see Christ's Body and Blood whether they partook or not, communion having become increasingly rare.

At the same time there was a multiplication of secondary devotions of a more or less private character, said by the priest silently at various points in the liturgy and overlaying its primitive structure. There was also great activity in the allegorical interpretation of the ceremonial actions.

All this went with an increased sense that the Mass was a sanctuary into which the priest entered alone, while the people stood in the outer court like the Jews of old in the temple. The custom grew up of saying the Canon silently, or in a subdued voice so that only the ministers in the sanctuary could hear it. The beginnings of this can be traced back to the period of Charlemagne, though the silent recitation of the Canon was never universal until Pius V established a uniform missal in 1570 after the Council of Trent.[1] The popular medieval tale of some shepherd boys who were struck by lightning for chanting the Canon in the open fields indicates contemporary notions. So also does the one addition to the Canon during this period : *'for whom we offer to thee or who offer this sacrifice of praise.'* The people are no longer thought of as offering the Eucharist as the People of God. It is the priest who offers it on their behalf. Even when the people received communion they did so only in one kind, being administered the wafer (no longer leavened bread after the eighth century), while the celebrant alone participated in the cup, for fear that some of the consecrated wine might be spilt

---

[1] Those who could prove that their local usage was at least two hundred years old were allowed to keep it. The ancient religious orders and the dioceses of Milan, Braga and Lyons still avail themselves of this permission today. There is also the use of the Mozarabic rite at Toledo (see p. 85 above) and the Uniate Churches are permitted to use their eastern rites.

in the administration. From the tenth century onwards the altar was pushed back against the wall of the church and the celebrant faced east instead of facing the people.

There were further developments in the latter part of the Middle Ages. (1) There was a multiplication of private masses and what twentieth-century slang might call a 'commercial racket' in them. This was one of the major abuses against which Luther and the Reformers fulminated. (2) The essential action of the Mass in the sung services came to be more and more separated from the singing of the choir and the devotions of the people, so that the priest proceeds to recite the Canon while the choir are still singing the *Sanctus*. In the Baroque period (seventeenth and eighteenth centuries) this led to the development of such elaborate musical accompaniment that celebrations became in effect sacred concerts, while the Mass itself was muttered remotely in the sanctuary. (3) A medieval development which is still as popular as ever in the Roman Church is the extra-liturgical devotions to the Blessed Sacrament, the consecrated Host (Latin : *hostia* = victim) being exposed in a 'monstrance' (even during the celebration of Mass itself) and honoured with genuflections which ultimately derive from the imperial court ceremonial. The popular Sunday evening service of Benediction is centred around this adoration of the Host exposed in the monstrance. This has developed from a growing concentration on the act of consecration rather than on the act of communion.

Though the Sacred Congregation of Rites established after the Council of Trent has for the most part through the centuries been content to make minor changes and clarify the rubrics, there has during the present century been a movement for liturgical reform known as the Liturgical Movement,[1] one of the many spiritual movements to which Rome has given

---

[1] For fuller accounts of this see A. G. Hebert, *Liturgy and Society* (London, Faber, 1935), L. Bouyer, *Life and Liturgy*, J. H. Srawley, *The Liturgical Movement*, A. R. Shands, *The Liturgical Movement and the Local Church*.

birth and which have influenced other Churches too. It aims at restoring the full participation of the people in the Mass, as in the early Church, when the celebrant faced the people across the altar with the latter closely grouped around it and actively taking their part in singing psalms, hymns and responses and in making the offertory. In some places celebrations facing the people are permitted. The more radical prophets of this movement advocate a thoroughgoing revision of the Mass-Liturgy and its use in the vernacular. So far its fruit has been mainly in the increased availability and use by the people of missals and other service books in their mother tongue while the service still goes on in Latin. They are encouraged to 'pray the Mass' rather than to pray their private devotions which were only partly connected with the Mass. Priests who are adherents of this movement normally administer to their people wafers which have been consecrated in the Mass in which they are participating, rather than taken from the Reserved Sacrament, which has been the regrettable practice hitherto. In sympathy with this movement the late Pope Pius XII in 1955 authorized valuable changes in the observance of Lent and Holy Week which return to a more primitive tradition. He relaxed the rules of fasting and authorized the celebration of Mass in the evening to enable the laity to receive communion more frequently, and gave general encouragement to the movement by officially sponsoring its principles in his encyclical of 1947, *Mediator Dei*. This encyclical, however, is also concerned to assert the validity of more conservative views and practices and to check the more radical manifestations of the movement.

THE THREE MODES OF MASS

There are three ways of celebrating the Mass :

1. *The Missa Solemnis,* or High Mass, in which the celebrant is assisted by a deacon and a subdeacon (parts which may be taken by men in priest's orders). A variation of this

is the Pontifical High Mass when a bishop is the celebrant. Both these derive in their ceremonial from the ancient stational Eucharist of the bishop in the main churches of his diocesan city.

2. *Missa Cantata,* or Sung Mass. This is the form usually taken by the main celebration of a Sunday or other important holy day in a parish church. This may be regarded as the modern counterpart of the presbyter's celebrations which were held in the lesser churches of the city in ancient times by delegation from the bishop.[1]

3. *Missa Lecta,* or Low Mass. There is nothing corresponding to this in the rites of the Eastern Churches, where every Eucharist is choral. When in the Middle Ages it became the custom for every priest to celebrate Mass daily and there was a multiplication of votive Masses, this mode of celebrating Mass was regarded as the norm and the *Missa Solemnis* and *Missa Cantata* as elaborations of it. Hence the fact that the manner of celebrating Holy Communion in the Churches of the Reformation corresponded most closely to the Low Mass. The Reformers also thought that its greater simplicity was more in accord with the primitive pattern of worship and closer to the simple Supper of the Upper Room.

In our generation many would decry this type of celebration, whether Anglican or Roman—the said service in the early morning at which the faithful few come to receive communion, while the majority (in the case of the Anglicans) attend Mattins or Evensong and, in the case of Roman Catholics, the *Missa Cantata* at a later hour without communicating. Rather, they say, there should be a parish Communion, as much choral as local musical talent will allow, which ought to be the main Sunday service attended by the

[1] In Rome until about the ninth century the Pope sent to each of the celebrants in the other churches of the city a fragment of bread which he had just consecrated at his own Mass. This *fermentum,* as it was called, was brought by an acolyte and mingled by the celebrant in his own consecrated chalice as a symbol of the unity in Christ of all the different congregations and their worship.

whole congregation with communicants receiving communion at it. Perhaps even more cogent is the criticism that the celebrant performs the rite almost entirely without the assistance of the congregation. This is true both of the Roman *Missa Lecta* and of its reformed counterparts.

There is much to be said for this view. The Eastern Churches celebrate their Eucharist after this manner as the main parochial act of worship; and modern revisions of the eucharistic liturgy in the Churches of the Reformation, such as those examined in chapter 7, have been drafted with this type of celebration in mind, though in them there is a simplicity which belongs to the reformed tradition.

On the other hand, there are those who defend the Low Mass (while not repudiating the other two modes) and its counterparts in the eucharistic tradition of the Churches of the Reformation as the legitimate heir to the house eucharists of the first three centuries. Domestic furniture and architecture were the pattern from which our Church furniture and architecture were derived and were also formative of the manner in which the Eucharist is celebrated. Why then should we abandon this mode of celebration which retains something of the quietness of a domestic rite?

In answer to this may we point out that the house Eucharist of the time of Ignatius of Antioch or Justin of Rome at which the bishop celebrated was intended for the whole congregation in a particular place and was therefore the parent of the *Missa Solemnis* as much as of the *Missa Lecta*. The hurried eucharists for small groups of the faithful in house or prison were the painful, if glorious, necessities of the Church undergoing persecution. And the private chapels of the great with their private chaplains, which appear even in the early centuries and were doubtless the connecting link between the house-eucharists of the days of persecution and the low masses of the Middle Ages, are hardly examples to be commended in our democratic age. The best that can be said for the Low Mass is that its evolution has provided a suitable mode of celebrating the Eucharist on such occasions as retreats and on week-days when only a few can be present. Also there will always be those—many of them among the saints—who will prefer a service which gives time for quiet contemplation to the parish Eucharist with its more demonstrative corporateness in worship. For these reasons the *Missa Lecta* and its reformed counterparts are not likely to die out, though greater participation by the congregation is to be desired and has in a measure been achieved wherever the influence of the liturgical movement has been felt.

THE CANON AND ITS MEANING

In all these three modes of celebrating Mass only the ceremonial and musical accompaniment differ. The text is identical and the invariable Canon is recited in the same way and accompanied by the same actions in every celebration. As the Canon is the key to the meaning of the Mass, we must study it in detail.

Defining it, as it was defined in the first seven centuries, rather than restricting it, as later, to the prayer after the *Sanctus,* we begin with :

1. *The Preface. Praefatio* originally meant a public declaration and in pre-Christian writers was used for the prayer which accompanied the sacrifice. In early Christian literature it may be used instead of the word 'Canon' to denote the whole eucharistic prayer; but in later usage it signifies only this introductory act of praise. The first words take up the last response of the people in the preceding dialogue : 'It is truly meet and right . . .'

In the early centuries there was a wealth of Proper Prefaces which are added after the introductory sentence of the common Preface and replace its latter half. The intention of these is to give particular point, in relation to the holy day or season being observed, to the general *eucharistia* (thanksgiving) for God's work in Christ. Many Roman Catholics

H

wish for a restoration of the primitive variety in Proper Prefaces on the ground that the Common Preface of the missal is somewhat restricted. Instead of sounding the note of thanksgiving for creation and redemption to be taken up again in the eucharistic prayer, which was doubtless the primitive tradition in the West, as it still is in the East, it is confined to the praise of the heavenly host and serves as little more than an introduction to the *Sanctus*.

2. *The Sanctus* (see pp. 54, 91).

3. *Te igitur*[1] ('Thee therefore...').

(a) *The request for acceptance of the gifts.*

The Roman rite differs from the Eastern and Gallican rites in offering up earthly gifts at the Offertory and in having this further plea for their acceptance followed by intercessory prayers immediately after the *Sanctus*. At this point the Eastern *anaphoras* normally take up again the theme of thanksgiving from the Preface with particular reference to Christ's incarnation and the redemption wrought by him.

However, though this beginning of the Roman prayer seems rather abrupt, we need not suppose that something has dropped out here. In the ancient world thanksgiving and sacrifice were closely related. Also we have a fragment of an Arian eucharistic prayer, apparently independent of the Roman Canon, which has a petition for the acceptance of the gifts in the same position and in similar terms.

This is already a prayer for consecration of the bread and wine : '... we humbly ask and beseech thee that thou wouldst deem acceptable and bless these gifts, these offerings, these holy unblemished sacrifices...'

Note the impressive *crescendo* (ascending sequence)—*dona* (a word used for any tokens of affection), *munera* (more formal and public presentations), *sacrificia* (offerings which man owes to God). There is indeed a larger *crescendo* of sacrificial

[1] The different paragraphs of the canon (as of other parts of the Mass liturgy) are known by the Latin words with which they begin. A literal translation of these words is given in brackets.

offering throughout the Canon of which this petition strikes the first note. There is no ground for the later theory of a moment of consecration at the Words of Institution : the consecration has already begun in this first paragraph.

(b) The beginning of the intercessions for the Church.

The gifts are offered for the universal Church and petition is made for its peace, welfare and unity, with special mention of the Pope and the bishop. The Roman Canon is unlike other eucharistic prayers in having intercessions before the Words of Institution as well as after. But we have good grounds for conjecturing that this and the following intercession have been inserted in the Canon since the fourth century.

4. *Memento, Domine* ('Remember, Lord . . .')—*The remembrance of the living.*

This too is related to the eucharistic offering. It expands the previous intercession with special reference to those present at the Mass which is being offered.

5. *Communicantes* ('In communion with . . .')—*The commemoration of and intercession through the saints.*

There is a parallel reference to the saints towards the end of the Canon. The commemoration here is remarkable for not being a complete sentence. Its ending, 'through the same Jesus Christ our Lord. Amen', suggests that it was originally a separate prayer inserted here.

6. *Hanc igitur* ('This oblation therefore . . .')—*The second request for acceptance.*

Again the conclusion, 'through Jesus Christ our Lord, Amen', suggests an interpolation. At one point it appears to have included special petitions on behalf of the offerers; and that may have been its original purpose. Now it reiterates the petition for the acceptance of the gifts, stresses that they are those of 'thy whole family', i.e., the whole Church—a truth which is stressed again later—and prays for peace in this life and salvation in the life to come.

7. *Quam oblationem* ('This oblation . . .')—*The third request for acceptance.*

This paragraph must be quoted in full :

Be pleased, O God, we beseech thee, to make this oblation in all things blessed, approved, valid, spiritual[1] and acceptable; that it may become for us the Body and Blood of thy most beloved Son our Lord Jesus Christ.

The smoothness of the Latin periods is here broken to introduce these five adjectives which give a legal emphasis to the formula characteristic of the Romans, even in their pre-Christian ritual formulas.

Though this prayer is now regarded as looking forward to the consecration at the Words of Institution, the repeated and legal emphasis of the five adjectives suggests that it may originally have been thought of as the formula of consecration. It would then be parallel to the *Epiklesis* (after the Words of Institution) in the Eastern rites. Another perhaps closer connexion is with the petition to fill the sacrifice with God's blessing which comes before the Words of Institution in the Egyptian liturgy.

8. *Qui pridie* ('Who on the day before . . .') and *Simili modo* ('in like manner . . .')—*The Narrative of the Institution.*

As in the Eastern liturgies, the narrative varies considerably from the biblical accounts. Though some of the non-biblical phrases are doubtless later devotional expansions (e.g., 'taking also this excellent chalice into his holy and venerable hands'), a phrase such as 'on the day before he suffered', which belongs to the Western tradition, instead of 'on the night in which he was betrayed', may well go back to a tradition which developed independently of the biblical texts and even before they were written.

[1] *Rationabilem* = Greek *logikon* as used in Rom. 12. 1, 1 Pet. 2. 2. But the prevalent interpretation gives it the meaning 'reasonable'.

9. *Unde et memores* ('And remembering therefore . . .')—
The Anamnesis and Oblation—Remembrance and offering.

In obedience to our Lord's command, just quoted, remembrance is made of his death, resurrection and ascension, and with the commemoration is linked the offering of the Victim, the elements on the altar now being declared the Body and Blood of Christ.

Two affirmations in this prayer call for particular attention :

(i) 'We thy servants, and indeed thy holy people, remembering the blessed passion . . . offer . . .'

There seems to be a distinction implied here between the ministry ('thy servants') and the laity ('thy holy people'), though a minority of Roman Catholics interpret 'thy servants' to mean the congregation here present and 'thy holy people' to mean the universal Church. Cranmer in the Anglican Prayer Book rightly obliterated this distinction by writing only 'we thy humble servants' in his post-communion prayer of oblation, though we may regret that he did not write 'we thy holy people'.

Some modern Roman Catholic theologians[1] are concerned to stress the importance of this emphatic *'and indeed (sed et)* thy holy people', which reiterates previous references to the offering of God's people, and make the concept of the *offering of the Church* the foundation of their eucharistic theology. The offering of Christ in the Mass is never something objectively separate from the Church. Rather he has chosen to ordain that his own self-offering should grow out of the offering of material gifts which are the product of the Church's daily labour, and this self-offering is made repeatedly present and consummated in the repetition of the rite which he has ordained, not only by liturgical actions of the ministers whom

---

1 E. G. M. de la Taille, *Mysterium Fidei* (1921; Eng. trans. *The Mystery of Faith*, London, Sheed & Ward) and J. A. Jungmann, *The Sacrifice of the Church* (London, Challoner Pubns., 1956), as well as in his great work, *The Mass of the Roman Rite*. This view is cautiously approved by the Pope in the encyclical *Mediator Dei* (see p. 102).

the Church on his authority has appointed, but also by the participaton of the people of God. Their self-offering in the consecration and above all in the communion is united with and fulfilled in his self-offering. Protestants may not agree with all that these writers say, but they can enter more easily into conversation with such doctrine than they can with the traditional Roman standpoint expressed in such statements as : 'Now mankind has a victim which God cannot refuse.'

(ii) The nature of the eucharistic sacrifice is defined (a) as God-given. Even the material elements of bread and wine are 'Thy gifts and presents'. (b) Supremely Christ in his self-offering is the Lamb which God has provided, 'a pure victim, a holy victim, an unspotted victim'. There is reference here both to the pure offering prophesied in Malachi and to the lamb without blemish of the Passover. The sacrifice is in the spiritual realm and not after the manner of pagan sacrifices. Moreover (c) in apposition to the thrice repeated word 'victim' are the words 'the holy bread of eternal life and the cup of everlasting salvation'. We have here a reference to the eucharistic teaching of John 6 which declares the eschatological character of the Eucharist, an eschatology both realized here and now to be fulfilled hereafter.

10 and 11. *Supra quae* ('Upon which . . .') and *Supplices te rogamus* ('We humbly beseech thee . . .')—*Further pleas for acceptance.*

These two prayers may be taken together. The first prays that God will look favourably upon the offered gifts, as he did upon the sacrifice of Abel, Abraham and Melchizedek. These are the Old Testament types who prefigure the People of God under the New Covenant : Abel the first man to be persecuted and martyred for righteousness' sake, Abraham the man of faith and father of Israel, Melchizedek the type of Christ's own High-priesthood who 'brought forth bread and wine' which was doubtless regarded by the compiler of this prayer as a sacrificial prefiguring of the Eucharist. The prayer seems

THE LITURGIES OF THE WEST

to imply that, even though the Church's offering is Christ himself, God can only accept it if it is offered with a faith and godliness of like character to that of these saints of old.

In the second prayer the language is even more figurative :

As suppliants we beseech thee, Almighty God, command these to be taken by the hands of thy holy Angel to thy heavenly altar in the presence of thy divine majesty; that as many of us as shall by partaking at this altar [literally : by this partaking of the altar] receive the most holy Body and Blood of thy Son may be filled with all heavenly benediction and grace. Through the same Christ our Lord. Amen.

The imagery of the heavenly tabernacle in the Epistle to the Hebrews is clearly in mind, and what the Church does in her worship on earth is envisaged as linked to the eternal Sacrifice in the realm of Heaven. It is from this altar on high[1] that the communicants partake of the spiritual gift of Christ's Body and Blood, a gift which the context implies must be received by faith. We may observe, too, that this consummation of the liturgical act of oblation *leads at once to mention of communion*. There is no justification whatever here for the later practice of non-communicating attendance.

Some have endeavoured to interpret this prayer as an equivalent of the Eastern *Epiklesis* and have even suggested that the angel who carries this gift to the heavenly altar is the Holy Spirit.[2] The truth is that we are dealing with a prayer couched in biblical language, but belonging to a period before the theological distinctions of the fourth century had been made. The 'angel' is the Old Testament angel of God's presence; but the altar belongs to the New Testament's interpretation of the Old. Also it is not a fourth century *Epiklesis* of consecration, but more akin to the early *Epiklesis* of communion which we find in Hippolytus and Sarapion.

1 This seems preferable to interpreting 'by partaking at this **altar**' as referring to the altar at which the Mass is being celebrated.
2 Others have suggested that he is Christ himself.

12. *Memento etiam* ('Remember also . . .')—*The remembrance of the dead.*

This prayer is not always found in the same position in the ancient texts. Doubtless it originally belonged to the remembrance of the living and the dead which was made before the Canon and was inserted when it became customary to have intercessions in the Canon. Though the association of this prayer with the saying of masses for the dead is reprehensible to many members of the reformed Churches, there is value in the reminder that the Church on earth is at one with the Church at rest in its eucharistic worship.

13. *Nobis quoque* ('To us also . . .')—*The fellowship of the saints.*

The celebrant says the words 'To us also thy sinful servants' aloud and strikes his breast. This is a strange survival from the time when the subdeacons had to get ready at this point to assist in the Fraction which followed. Although, after the introduction of wafers instead of bread, their assistance was no longer required, the signal was still given in this way and an allegorical interpretation was attached to it as representing the confession of the centurion at the cross and the striking of the breast by those who witnessed the crucifixion.

Probably the 'sinful servants' are the celebrant and his fellow ministers, though the phrase is generally extended to mean the whole congregation. Again in this final prayer we are brought face to face with both a present reality and a final hope. We look forward to the consummation hereafter of our fellowship with the Church triumphant here and now.

14. *The Doxology.*

This has become somewhat confused and seems to be a combination of two formulas. The former of these probably belongs to the blessing of gifts in kind made at the offertory. *The Apostolic Tradition* of Hippolytus had a separate blessing of these outside the Canon, but the blessing may have been introduced into the Canon for the same reason as that for the introduction of the intercessory prayers, i.e., that it would be more efficacious if given 'in the presence of the sacred mysteries'. This blessing has now disappeared, but a vestige of the formula still remains. On only one occasion in the year oil is consecrated by the Bishop for the unction of the sick. This is done on Maundy Thursday and the words of consecration are inserted at this very point—another example of 'the preservation of that which is ancient in a season liturgically of high value'.

In spite of the lack of coherence we have noted, as resulting from the insertion of prayers at different times and their imperfect co-ordination, there can be discerned in the Canon of the Mass an overall unity, which can best be illustrated diagrammatically as a pyramid the apex of which is the Narrative of the Institution, the other prayers in their order being represented by steps leading up to it and down from it, the prayers and action of the Church thus finding their climax in the command and example of our Lord himself.

Or alternatively we may be helped in our understanding of the Canon by dividing it into three broad divisions :

The first commends to God the oblation of bread and wine offered for consecration, and makes a brief intercessory mention of the Church, the Pope and the Bishop, together with a commemoration of the Blessed Virgin, the Apostles and other saints; the second prays for the blessing of the oblation, that it may become Christ's Body and Blood, and effects consecration through the Institution Narrative, ending with the words, 'As often as ye shall do this, ye shall make the memorial of me'; in the third division the consecrated Oblation is offered to the Divine Majesty, a short prayer is said on behalf of the dead, and the whole concludes with a petition that the worshippers may be admitted to the fellowship of the saints.[1]

The Mass stresses the aspect of offering to the neglect of

1 Quoted from E. C. Ratcliff's lecture, *The Liturgical Work of Archbishop Cranmer.*

other important elements in our eucharistic worship, particularly that of thanksgiving. This one-sidedness doubtless gave
rise to the distortions of doctrine and practice which appeared
in the Middle Ages; but its central eucharistic prayer is not
only pre-medieval, but contains within it elements which are
probably more primitive in form than their counterparts in
other ancient liturgies. Though the Reformers for many
reasons were constrained to abandon it or radically to recast
it, it may now be studied by their descendants as a classic of
eucharistic devotion which cannot be altogether confined
within the bounds of official Roman doctrine as defined at the
Council of Trent.

ECCLESIASTICAL DISCIPLINE

From the earliest times the Church has been concerned to
guard its common life and particularly its eucharistic worship
from the corruption of sin. We have evidence of public
confession and the fencing of the table in the *Didache,* and in
the account of Christian worship recorded by Pliny at the
beginning of the second century (see p. 47).

This developed during the course of the first three centuries
into a regular public discipline which, however, was concerned
with the graver sins rather than with minor offences. At first
rigorism prevailed, inspired perhaps by the teaching of the
Epistle to the Hebrews. Anyone who committed a grievous
sin after baptism was deemed to have cut himself off from the
fellowship of the Church. Hence the tendency, revealed, for
instance, in the writings of Tertullian, to postpone baptism as
late as possible. Even as late as the fourth century we find
the Emperor Constantine receiving baptism only on his death-
bed, though this was probably exceptional.

While those who had been baptized might be allowed one
restoration after penance in the case of most heinous sins,
exception was in the early centuries made in the case of
murder, adultery and apostasy, for which at first there was

no reconciliation. One of the major historical issues of the Church's life in the early centuries is the battle between rigorism and charity in which the latter eventually won. Indeed rigorism (though it may have saved the Church at the end of the first century) very nearly led to its annihilation in the Decian persecution of the middle of the third century, when the persecuting authorities realized that they had only to persuade a person accused of being a Christian to commit a trivial act of apostasy to ensure that he was excommunicated for life. The Church changed its policy just in time and so was able to survive this and the still more severe persecution of Diocletian at the beginning of the fourth century, but not without many of the rigorists being driven into schism under the leadership of Novatian and of Donatus.

The public penance for sin (*exhomologesis*) after confession included a series of demonstrations of penitence such as the wearing of sackcloth and ashes, fasting, prostration before the ministry, and kneeling before the laity. In Syria (see the account of the *Liturgy of the Apostolic Constitutions,* pp. 60-61) the penitents were dismissed along with the catechumens before the Eucharist proper began. More commonly in the West and in other parts of the East they were only excluded from reception of communion. Maundy Thursday was the traditional day for the restoration of penitents to communion after absolution by the Bishop. In some places penitentiary priests were appointed to exercise the ministry of absolution, particularly during the later persecutions when a large number of apostates were eager to be restored. By the fifth and sixth centuries the parochial clergy had largely taken over this responsibility, and at the same time the last vestige of rigorism —the rule that only one reconciliation could be allowed to a grievous sinner—was abandoned. General absolutions were also given on other days than Maundy Thursday. In the early Middle Ages the practice adopted in the monasteries of periodical confession began to spread to the laity. By the thirteenth century it was so well established everywhere that the Fourth Lateran Council (1215) made the practice of private confession before communion compulsory, as it is in the Roman Church to this day. This perhaps marks a change of emphasis from the public worship of the Church, as the corporate action of the people of God, to the individual's private relationship with God.[1]

Also to the Middle Ages belongs the introduction of acts of confession into the Liturgy itself, these being absent from the earliest texts. In the Roman rite there is the *Confiteor* (I confess) in which celebrant and ministers confess to and are absolved by each other at the beginning of the Mass. There are also the private prayers said by the celebrant, particularly the devotions immediately before communion, which are of a confessional character. Similar devotions are prescribed for the people, notable among these being the general confession in the vernacular after the sermon used in the churches of Germany from the ninth century onwards, which doubtless had influence on the forms of confession in the churches of the Reformation.

Consciousness of sin can be carried to the point of morbid scrupulosity, as is witnessed by the multiplication of confessional prayers and the extravagant language used in some of them in the medieval texts of the Mass. Similar exaggeration can be observed in the products of the Reformation. On the other hand, there is the danger that the Church's discipline may become too easy and confession a mere verbal form. The sacrament of Holy Communion is for sinners; but they can only approach it worthily if they do so in penitence and faith.

[1] The early manner of absolution was by prayer to God for forgiveness or the expression of a wish. The formula 'I absolve thee', only came in in the thirteenth century under the influence of Thomas Aquinas and others.

CHAPTER 7

HOLY COMMUNION IN THE CHURCHES OF THE REFORMATION

INTRODUCTORY

THE crisis in worship of the Reformation which manifested itself in the repudiation by the Reformers of the Roman Mass was in many ways central to the whole religious upheaval of the time; for the Reformers believed that if they could get rid of the Mass the many evils which were corrupting the life of the Church would be swept away with it, and doctrine and life, as well as worship, would be restored to their primitive purity. At the same time this liturgical revolution must be viewed against the wider background of theological trends and social and political issues with which it was closely related in a single historical complex. For this the student is referred to the standard histories of the period and to the writings of the Reformers themselves, particularly of Luther and Calvin in Europe and of Hooker in England.

The Reformation and its fruits inevitably provoke a clash of contrary opinions, and it is difficult for any writer on the subject to be impartial. Nevertheless, there are some observations both of approval and of criticism which may reasonably claim agreement from those of contrasting points of view.

1. Even those of a 'catholic' standpoint, whether Roman or Anglican, admit that decadence and distortion had overtaken the eucharistic worship of the West during the Middle Ages.

(a) The Eucharist had ceased to be the corporate action of the whole congregation and had come to be regarded as the sacerdotal action of the celebrant alone.

(b) Each celebration of the Mass was regarded as a separate sacrificial offering which, though related to Calvary, had a value and efficacy of its own which could be applied, according to the intention of the celebrant, to particular souls or causes.

(c) It is probably true that until the fourteenth century none of the younger European languages was capable of providing a suitable medium for public worship. All were in very rudimentary stages of development and might be described as collections of local dialects rather than languages. Latin was therefore the only suitable instrument for the unification of the Church's worship, in the same way as it was the common medium of western European culture. But now the other European languages had come into their own and began to produce literature, while even before this happened Latin had long ceased to be understood by the uneducated. The time was ripe for translations of the Liturgy; but the unreformed Church was either unable or unwilling to grant these to the people, who had to be content with devotions in their own language of a more or less private character to be used at the Mass, rather than with a comprehensible rendering of the Mass itself.

(d) The laity was thus deprived of any participation in the rite, even that of hearing it in their own tongue. Their devotional impulses were therefore concentrated on *seeing* it performed, particularly on seeing the elevation after the consecration, which had been introduced in the twelfth century for this very purpose. Thus the Words of Institution ceased to be thought of as one integral part in the whole sequence of the Eucharist from offertory to communion and were regarded instead as the climax in which the words and actions of the priest alone effected the eucharistic presence which the people had come to adore. And, starved as they were of a genuine ministry of the Word which would enable them to understand the ministry of the Sacraments, their adoration was inevitably mixed with gross superstition.

(e) Although the Canon of the Mass still retained its ancient *Anamnesis* not only of the Passion, but also of the Resurrection and Ascension, and had emphatic eschatological reference, as we have seen, in the figure of the heavenly altar and the offering of the 'bread of eternal life and the cup of everlasting salvation', medieval devotion neglected these aspects and concentrated on the historical event of the crucifixion. We see this particularly in the private prayers of the celebrant with which the Mass-liturgy became overlaid. All this was connected with the notion of Christ's sacrifice as limited to his death and therefore an historical event of the past, which could only be made present by being repeated sacramentally on the altar.[1]

We may regret the violence of language and action with which the break with the old tradition was made, remembering, however, that there was violence on both sides and that bottled-up emotions when released were liable to lead to this. But there can be no doubt that the liturgical practice of the time cried out for reform, and the turbulent way in which the reform came was a divine judgment on an unrepentant Church.

From the point of view of liturgical history alone the reformers had right on their side when they revolted against liturgical fixity. Whether Gregory the Great's phrase, 'a prayer which a schoolmaster composed', denotes the Canon of the Mass (as would seem the most obvious interpretation in the context of his letter) or some other prayer which followed it and has since disappeared, as Roman liturgists are inclined to think, the Canon as we know it was only one formulation of the Roman liturgical tradition which happened to attain fixity and permanent authorization. If the transition from the fluid rite to the fixed rite had taken place a hundred

---

1 For a fuller exposition of these points see Dix, *Shape of the Liturgy*, ch. xvi. The more detailed studies of Jungmann, though less explicitly critical of the medieval development, imply very much the same judgment.

years earlier or later the formulation might have been very different. In view of the ineptitude of the interpolations and dislocations which occurred in the Canon at the hands of blundering papal liturgists even after it had attained fixity, it may be well that it remained largely unchanged for a thousand years. But there was every precedent in its primitive history for revision at much more frequent intervals, and above all in the third- or fourth-century change from Greek to Latin in Rome a precedent for translation into other languages. The liturgical work of the reformers was to this extent in accord with the most ancient liturgical tradition. One of the tragic fruits of controversy was that the reaction of the Roman hierarchy to this was to enforce an even more rigid fixity than before. Gregory's dictum, 'In the unity of faith the varied usage of the Church does not matter', had been forgotten.

Above all the Reformation was a rediscovery of the congregation. Even when we read Reformation rites which seem to have rejected unnecessarily the classical heritage of worship, we must not forget the vigour of congregational understanding and participation which they presuppose. This in itself was a liturgical revival and a renewal of the understanding of one aspect of the nature of the Church.

2. On the other hand, Protestants who have studied the early history of Christian worship and also know something of the Eastern liturgies may well agree in some measure with Dix's contention that the reformers were 'post-medieval' in their thinking, i.e., conditioned by lines of thought and practice which had developed during the Middle Ages. Although they revolted against these, they could not altogether free themselves from their influence. Although they knew that the liturgy ought to be understood by the people and culminate in the communion in both kinds, they knew no example to guide them in their revision of it other than the Mass itself, and that in its late medieval form. Hence the limitations and defects of their liturgical work. In particular they inherited the individualism of the medieval period and so were inclined

to regard communion as the devotional act of the believer rather than the corporate act of the Church. They were also bound by the view of Christ's sacrifice as limited to his death, so that in rejecting the notion of a repetition of that sacrifice in the Eucharist they had no alternative but to regard the Eucharist as a mere remembering of that death, the benefits of which the believer appropriated by faith. They could not be blamed for this, for it is only as a result of recent biblical studies that we have come to understand the fulness of biblical sacrifice[1] as including the whole sequence of (a) obedience to the divine command in offering the sacrificial victim, (b) the death of the victim as one stage, though the central one, in the sacrifice, and (c) finally the use made of the sacrifice by offering to God through fire on the altar and, in the case of certain types of offering, by communion-fellowship between the worshippers and God in the sacrificial meal. If this had been understood in the sixteenth century, the truth of the uniqueness and unrepeatable character of Christ's sacrifice could have been conserved, while recognizing that the Eucharist was still sacrificial in character as being the means whereby the people of God both appropriated Christ's sacrifice and, in union with him, offered themselves to the Father. There is evidence in Luther's sermons that his Augustinian background led him to retain something of this concept in his teaching; but his controversy with Rome and his denunciation of the sacrifice of the Mass prevented his developing it in his reformed Mass. Also, as we shall see, the Anglican rite allows in some measure this interpretation; but the general tendency was to banish all mention of sacrifice from the liturgy.

All this should be a salutary reminder to us that reformed orders of worship are no more sacrosanct than the Mass, particularly now that biblical and liturgical studies have provided us with a wealth of material for their revision and

[1] See F. C. N. Hicks, *The Fulness of Sacrifice* (London, S.P.C.K., 1946)

I

enrichment. Additional factors which should inspire us to boldness in the venture are that the meaning of words changes and forms of thought are for ever in transition. The liturgical products of the sixteenth century may therefore be almost as remote from the life of the Church in the twentieth as were the products of the fourth century in the sixteenth. Still more is it true that forms of worship devised for a nominally Christian Europe are likely to need considerable adaptation and enrichment from local sources if they are to fit the situation of the Church in Asia or Africa. Those members of the younger Churches who would like to see the prayer books imported for them from abroad by the pioneer missionaries of their area retained without change or adaptation should reflect on the consequences of this attitude in the past.

THE LUTHERAN RITES

There has been a widespread return to Luther among Protestant theologians outside the Lutheran Churches and a recognition that the first of the reformers was also theologically the most original and creative of them all. In his dealing, however, with the worship of the Church he seems to have been torn between a desire to make bold and drastic change in accordance with his doctrinal convictions, and a conservative adherence to the traditional rites and ceremonies which was closely linked with his opposition to the teaching and practice of Carlstadt and Zwingli and his fear that vital religious values would be lost if their interpretation of the Eucharist were to prevail.

At first Luther hesitated to depart from the traditional Latin, and his *Formula Missae* of 1523 is simply the old Roman Mass with the ceremonial retained at least optionally, but with 'sacrificial' references excised This involved a ruthless treatment of the Liturgy of the Faithful. The offertory is abandoned and the elements are placed on the table during the Creed. Though the *Sursum corda* and prefaces are retained, the Words of Institution are placed between the preface and the *Sanctus*. The *Benedictus qui venit* ('Blessed is he that cometh . . .') follows, during which there is an elevation. The rest of the Canon is omitted (which means amongst other things that there are no intercessions in the whole rite) and the Lord's Prayer and the 'Peace' follow, after which communion is given during the singing of the *Agnus Dei* and a communion psalm, as in the old rite. After the post-communion prayer the service ends with the Aaronic Blessing (Numbers 6. 24-26) which was soon in common use in reformed worship.

His German Mass (*Deudsche Messe*) of 1526, while it still retained vestments, lights, and altars 'for the time', was more drastic in its treatment of the traditional rite on which it was based. Some changes we may welcome : the introduction of German hymns in place of the *Introit, Gradual* and *Alleluia,* and the making of a sermon obligatory. The ministry of the Word was reasserted and the foundations laid by Luther himself of the rich heritage of German hymnody. But instead of the Offertory there is a paraphrase of the Lord's Prayer and a short exhortation. Consecration is by recital of the Words of Institution, the rest of the Canon being abolished. During the communion the *Sanctus* or *Agnus Dei* may be sung in German or replaced by a German hymn. After communion comes Luther's own collect 'We thank thee, Almighty Lord God . . .' and the Aaronic Blessing.

LATER REVISIONS

Lutherans have never stressed uniformity in worship, and in consequence Lutheran liturgical forms have been numerous and have varied considerably. There is a recognizable common heritage in all Lutheran eucharistic rites, derived in part from Luther's own liturgical experiments and in part from his conservative retention of elements in the western liturgical tradition.

This was even more manifest a generation ago than it is today, where in Germany, Sweden or America Lutheran service books all followed Luther in abbreviating the eucharistic prayer in one way or another. The rite of the Church of Sweden, for instance, had the Words of Institution, the Lord's Prayer, the *Sanctus*. In the 1919 edition of the *Common Service Book* of the United Lutheran Church in America the order was: the Sanctus, the Lord's Prayer, the Words of Institution. There had been some movement away from the radical severity of the sixteenth century, so that almost all variations from Luther's rite of 1526 were in the direction of restoration and enrichment.

THE REVISED SWEDISH RITE

But such minor amendments were not enough to satisfy those who had been influenced by the liturgical revival, which began to have its effect in the Lutheran Churches as in other communions.   The morning star of liturgical reform was Yngve Brilioth, later to become Bishop and Archbishop, who as a young professor of ecclesiastical history wrote his epoch-making *Eucharistic Faith and Practice, Evangelical and Catholic* (1926; English edition 1930). The desire for reform expressed in this book led to a revision of the Swedish Mass in 1937.

As in the older order there is an opening hymn and a preparatory act of confession and prayer for forgiveness, which on certain festivals is preceded by an Introit. Then follows the *Kyrie* ('Lord have mercy upon us . . .') and the *Gloria in excelsis* ('Glory to God in the highest . . .').

The ministry of the Word begins with the salutation and response ('The Lord be with you': 'And with thy spirit') and continues with the Collect for the day, Epistle, Gradual, Gospel, Creed, and Sermon followed by a prayer. An offertory sentence is said and the collection taken; but there is no preparation of the bread and wine at this point.   The service of the Word concludes with a general prayer for the church of which there are varying forms.

A hymn follows during which the elements are prepared. Then comes the *Sursum Corda*, etc.   Instead of only two prefaces as formerly there are now four: (i) a general preface based on the Roman proper preface for Easter; (ii) a Christmas preface; (iii) a Lenten preface, giving thanks for Christ's death for 'us who are worthy of death'; (iv) a Trinity preface, not specifically concerned with the Trinity, but referring to Christ as 'the living Bread which came down from heaven'.

Following this enrichment of the prefaces there has been some restoration of the canon which now runs:

Sanctus (including *Benedictus qui venit*)

Prayer of thanksgiving for the gift of salvation through Christ, and

Prayer for the sending of the Holy Spirit into our hearts 'that he may kindle in us a living faith'.

Words of Institution

Lord's Prayer

The *Pax* ('The peace of the Lord be with you')

The *Agnus Dei* (sung while the priest holds the consecrated bread)

The communion is followed by Luther's Post-Communion collect, 'We thank thee, almighty Lord God', a versicle and response of thanksgiving and the Aaronic blessing.

THE LITURGY OF THE FEDERATION OF LUTHERAN CHURCHES IN INDIA

The Swedish revision may be classed as conservative in that it has only partly restored the ancient eucharistic prayer and remains within the liturgical tradition of the Lutheran reformation. There are, however, essays in Lutheran liturgical revision which have gone further. One of these deserving consideration is the liturgy adopted by the Federation of Lutheran Churches in India in 1935 for optional use. It is evidently the fruit of the desire for a restoration of the classical shape of the liturgy to which Brilioth had given expression, but, as has been the case in the Anglican Communion, a younger branch of the Church was able to be more radical than the mother Church.

The first part of the service (corresponding to the ancient

liturgy of the catechumens) introduces an optional Old Testament lesson after which is said the *Trisagion* from the Eastern rites. The Offertory is also restored to its full emphasis.

The second part of the service, corresponding to the Liturgy of the Faithful, begins with a prayer of Luther based upon the words of the centurion : 'Lord I am not worthy . . .' which are used in the Roman rite immediately before Communion. Though different in wording it is not dissimilar in meaning to the Anglican prayer of humble access.

The eucharistic prayer has borrowed some elements from Eastern *anaphoras*. The *Sursum corda* is preceded by the Pauline grace, as in the Eastern liturgies, instead of the Egyptian and Western salutation. This opening dialogue is followed by the Preface, Proper Preface, *Sanctus, Benedictus qui venit,* and a commemoration of the incarnation and redemption abbreviated from the *Liturgy of St. James.* The narrative of the Institution which comes next is followed by the *Anamnesis* and Oblation and by an *Epiklesis.*

The *Epiklesis* is :

And, we beseech thee, send down Thy Holy Spirit upon us and upon these gifts here before Thee, that according to the Word of Thy dear Son they may be sanctified and blessed, that this bread may be the Body of Christ and this wine His precious Blood, that all, who in true faith and with contrite hearts eat and drink thereof to the remission of sins, may be sanctified in soul and body, that we may be one body and one spirit, and may have our portion with all Thy saints who have been well-pleasing unto Thee, through Jesus Christ our Lord.

The service proceeds as follows :

The Lord's Prayer with protocol and embolism.
The Pax ('The peace of the Lord be with you alway').
The *Agnus Dei.*
The Administration of Communion.
The *Nunc Dimittis* (Simeon's Hymn).

The Thanksgiving.
Dialogue as in the American rite.
Benediction.

Comparison with the eucharistic prayers in *The Order of the Lord's Supper* in the Church of South India and the Order of the Holy Eucharist in the revised Prayer Book of the Church of India, Burma, Pakistan and Ceylon (Anglican) will reveal remarkable affinities. The liturgical committees of the three Churches, which in any case carried out their work at different times, appear to have had little if any liaison with each other apart from correspondence with individuals; but all three appear to have had the same inspiration to draw upon the liturgical heritage of the East (in this case the Syrian heritage established in the country for many centuries) as well as upon the heritage imported more recently from the West. It would not be an exaggeration to say that during the past two decades this threefold liturgical development, which happens to have taken place in India, is of more than merely Indian significance. This fusion of heritages, Eastern and Western, may be a signpost for the future—and not in the realm of worship alone.

REVISION IN AMERICA—THE LITURGY OF 1958

The great union of the majority of Lutheran Churches in the U.S.A. which took place in 1962 was preceded by a co-operative enterprise in liturgical revision in which the uniting Churches and Lutherans in Canada took part. It resulted in the publication in 1958 of the new *Service Book and Hymnal*, a far-reaching revision which manifests similar tendencies in its Common Liturgy to those found in the Indian revision we have just studied.

The former American rite was not dissimilar to the revised Swedish rite which we have examined briefly above. The most significant enrichments of the eucharistic order are: (i) a restoration in brief form of the ancient litany associated with the *Kyrie eleison* ('Lord have mercy') near the beginning of the service; (ii) a revision of the *Pericopes* (Epistles and

Gospels) together with the addition of Old Testament lessons, holy days hitherto unobserved, and new proper prefaces for Advent and All Saints' Day; (iii) an entirely new text of the Prayer for the Church in litany form; (iv) a eucharistic prayer which is admirable in its brevity and includes commemoration of the incarnation and redemption, the Words of Institution, *Anamnesis* and *Epiklesis*, followed by the Lord's Prayer; one may regret that the minister says most of this last alone, and the people only join in at 'For Thine is the Kingdom . . .'[1]

THE RITES OF THE REFORMED CHURCHES

It was one of the sad fruits of the Reformation that differences among the leading reformers soon led to divisions amongst their followers in addition to their common secession from Rome. Except for the Anglican *Book of Common Prayer*, which will be given separate consideration, other liturgical products of the Reformation advanced further in a Protestant direction than did Luther and were more radical in their departure from Roman tradition than he. Indeed Luther and the Anglicans were accused of a superstitious and illogical adherence to the old ways.

As a great variety of orders for the Lord's Supper was produced in the sixteenth century and a still greater multiplicity since, it will not be possible to study them all in detail. Also, as the movement of the Reformation advanced, the right of the minister to use extempore prayer in all services became established, and printed forms were regarded only as general guides or outlines for him to follow rather than as prescribed texts which he was obliged to read word for word. This was a return in one respect to the fluid rite of the first three centuries; but it means that any particular service book, sixteenth century or modern, is direct evidence only for the theological and liturgical opinions of the compiler or compilers and less

[1] For further details see the essay, 'New Features of Recent Lutheran Liturgy in America', by L. D. Reed in *Studia Liturgica* I. 1 (March 1962).

certain evidence for the common mind of the Church at that time.

We may select a few of these forms of celebrating the Lord's Supper for comment.

1. *Zwinglian rites.*

Zwingli of Zurich may have been less at variance than is sometimes supposed with Luther and Calvin in his teaching concerning the Lord's Supper; but, brought up in the new humanism of the Renaissance rather than in medieval scholasticism like Luther and Calvin, he was more rationalistic in his approach and did not regard the Lord's Supper as anything more than the act of a congregation confessing its faith. His first German rite appeared in Zurich in 1525 and became the exemplar for later Zwinglian worship. In its simplicity of structure, as well as in its theology, it has undoubtedly influenced much Protestant worship in subsequent generations. The service as a whole tends to be didactic rather than devotional, a characteristic not infrequently found elsewhere in the rites of this period. Unlike Luther and Calvin who fought unsuccessfully for weekly celebrations of Holy Communion, Zwingli ordained that Communion should only be given four times a year. Here is the beginning of the process by which the Eucharist ceased to be the norm of Sunday worship in most Protestant churches.

There was, however, a positive element in Zwingli's conception of the Eucharist, which has been very influential in the reformed administration of Communion, including the Anglican, and on church architecture in the post-Reformation period. This was his presentation of Communion as a corporate occasion, the Church's family meal around a table. We find this reasserted with varying emphasis in the liturgical movements of our time. Even if in other respects we regard Zwingli's teaching and practice in the Lord's Supper as an impoverishment, in this respect he undoubtedly enriched eucharistic worship by his reassertion of an element in the worship of the early Church.

2. *The rites of Strasbourg and Geneva*

Strasbourg, where Lutheran teaching was modified by the Zwinglian Bucer and which later received the ministry of Calvin, was, as far as worship is concerned, the most creative centre of the Reformation, and from it issued a series of liturgical revisions which were to have far-reaching influence on the Churches of the Reformation.

Of particular note is the German rite of 1537 which owes its form to the work of Bucer. Calvin's French rites of Strasbourg and Geneva are derived from it and it was also the model for the Scottish rite. It may therefore be regarded as the parent rite of the Reformed tradition of eucharistic worship. Calvin simplified it by having only one form of confession and one intercession and consecration prayer, modelling his forms on one of the alternatives provided by Bucer. Less happy changes made by him were the introduction of a tedious paraphrase of the Lord's Prayer and a metrical form of the Decalogue. John Knox's *The Forme of Prayers* or *Book of Common Order,* originally printed in Geneva, was immediately indebted to Calvin's revision of his Strasbourg rite at Geneva, though it is not a slavish translation.

The order of the Strasbourg rite of 1537 :

The Liturgy of the Word
   Confession
   Scriptural word of pardon (1 Timothy 1. 15)
   Declaration of forgiveness
   Psalm, hymn, or 'Lord have mercy'
   and *Gloria in excelsis.*
(For these Calvin substituted the Decalogue with 'Lord have mercy upon us' as a response, though he replaced it in the Genevan rite by a metrical Psalm.)
   Collect for illumination
   Metrical Psalm
   Lection (Gospel)
   Sermon followed by printed exhortation

The Liturgy of the Upper Room

    Collection of alms
    Preparation of elements while Apostles' Creed is sung
    Intercessions and consecration prayer (a very long prayer)
    Lord's Prayer
    Exhortation
    Words of Institution
    Fraction
    Delivery
    Communion while a psalm or hymn is sung
    Post-communion collect
    Aaronic blessing and Dismissal[1]

3. *The Reformed Churches today*

Modern reformed service books may have more than one alternative rite, e.g., the present *Book of Common Order* of the Church of Scotland. This is in part a recognition of differing liturgical traditions (the old Free Church as well as the established Church) within the Church; in part it allows for the fact that different modes of liturgy may be suitable for different types of congregations and different occasions. The current edition of *The Book of Common Order* will repay careful study as a product which, while remaining in the Genevan tradition, has modified some of the more forbidding aspects of Reformation worship and also recovered something of the classical heritage. In fact it is the product of a liturgical revival which has its affinities with the Anglican one.

The Book of Common Order of the United Church of Canada, as the product of a union of Churches which hopes eventually to include the Anglican Church of Canada and has therefore endeavoured to do justice to the Anglican heritage in its worship, is one of the most significant liturgical achievements of our time. Its order for Holy Communion should be compared with *The Order for the Lord's Supper* of the Church of South India.

[1] For a fuller account of this rite and a translation of most of it see Maxwell, *An Outline of Christian Worship,* pp. 101-115.

Another fine product is *A Book of Public Worship,* compiled by four British Congregational ministers for the guidance of their brethren, which is not dissimilar in its eucharistc worship to the alternative forms in the Scottish *Book of Common Order.* The student, in whatever part of the world he dwells, will find service books to provide him with examples of this widespread tradition which, being more fluid than that of the ancient Churches or the Anglican Communion, has been able to adapt itself more easily to local conditions.

These service books with their many variations of eucharistic worship owe much to the Puritan tradition which has been dominant in the English Free Churches and in the majority of Churches in the U.S.A. The positive emphases of this tradition are : (*a*) freedom of the Spirit in worship (hence the prevailing use of extempore prayer); (*b*) forms of worship based on the Bible and having as their centre the declaration of the Word of God in the reading of Scripture and preaching; (*c*) congregations of the faithful grounded and disciplined in this scripturally based worship. As the introduction to *A Book of Public Worship* puts it :

> Modern Congregationalists will not be bludgeoned or beguiled into a conformity which their fathers resisted unto blood. Yet it is a cardinal error to think of the early Congregationalists as liturgical anarchists. They pleaded—and paid—for their liberty; but their worship was orderly. They were concerned, not that they might do as they pleased, but that they might worship as they ought. Standards of worship could not be fixed by the State; they had been determined by the Gospel.

Those who adhere to the classical forms of liturgical worship have still to learn to appreciate the importance of this contribution to the revival of worship, though some measure of appreciation can be discerned in the liturgical movements of our time.

THE ANGLICAN RITES

It should not be offensive to those who are not Anglicans to claim that no liturgical composer of the Reformation can compare in stature with Archbishop Thomas Cranmer, the architect of the English *Book of Common Prayer*.[1]

Cranmer's creative genius did not depend upon originality, which may not always be an advantage in liturgical composition. He was concerned to preserve as much of the old rites as possible, and much of the Prayer Book consists of free translation from the Roman service books. Also others of the reformers had pioneered before him. In the years 1531-2, when he was English ambassador to the Emperor Charles V immediately before becoming Archbishop of Canterbury, he had come in contact with Lutheran worship, and we have a direct report (from his predecessor as ambassador, Sir Thomas Elyot) of his attendance at a Lutheran Mass in Nuremberg. There is no doubt that he made lasting friendships among the continental reformers. One of his first essays in English liturgical writing, *The Order of the Communion*, published in 1548, was based on *A Simple and Religious Consultation* (*Simplex et pia deliberatio*) which had been written in German by Melanchthon and Bucer and issued by Archbishop Hermann of Cologne, the English version being published in 1547. The devotion in preparation for Communion which Cranmer

1 For evidence that the Prayer Book is substantially Cranmer's work see E. C. Ratcliff, 'The Liturgical Work of Archbishop Cranmer', one of the three commemorative lectures in a booklet, *Thomas Cranmer* (London, Church Information Board, 1956; Ratcliff's lecture also published in the *Journal of Ecclesiastical History*, October, 1956). This lecture contains a wealth of information to which this chapter is at several points indebted.

Standard works on *The Book of Common Prayer* are: F. Procter and W. H. Frere, *A New History of the Book of Common Prayer* (London, Macmillan, 1901), F. E. Brightman, *The English Rite*, M. H. Shepherd, *The Oxford American Prayer Book Commentary* (New York, O.U.P., 1950). Maxwell has a useful chapter on the English and Scottish Prayer Books.

For Cranmer's eucharistic theology see F. M. Powicke, *The Reformation In England* (London, O.U.P., 1941). Dix's unsympathetic treatment of Cranmer in *The Shape of the Liturgy* is partly based on Powicke's conclusions.

derived from it contained the exhortation to confession, confession, absolution, comfortable words and prayer of humble access which are still to be found in the Anglican rite with only slight verbal alterations, though differently arranged. Cranmer's original intention was that they should be used immediately before the communion of the people in the Latin Mass and he included them in the same position in his first English rite of 1549. His rubric in the 1549 rite that at the offertory the communicants should come to the front ('tarry in the choir or in some convenient place nigh the choir'), was also derived from this source. But a comparison of the two texts leaves no doubt that he has greatly improved on his exemplar. Similarly the introductory sentence (protocol) to the Lord's Prayer, 'As our Saviour Christ hath commanded and taught us, we are bold to say', is a translation of the German revision of the Latin sentence found in the Lutheran Order of Electoral Brandenburg. The use of exhortations or addresses to the people for their instruction was copied from the continental reformers, and the general structure of the service and its principle that the people should take part, 'as in the usages of the primitive Church', owed much to the Lutheran form of worship. Cranmer however showed his independence of the Lutherans in his retention of the Canon of the Mass, or rather his re-writing of it to give expression to Reformation doctrine, rather than mutilating it in a negative manner as Luther had done.

A distinction of Cranmer's work is the excellence of his literary style, which is perfectly suited to liturgy. It was no mean task to give to the Prayer Book, compiled as it was from various sources, a uniform style, and Cranmer's work must take its place as a literary classic alongside the King James Version of the Bible and the plays of Shakespeare which belong to the same golden age of English literature. Even in translation into foreign languages something of the majesty of Cranmer's prose survives, and there is no doubt that English-speaking Churches of other than Anglican heritage

have often looked to the *Book of Common Prayer* as a model
of liturgical writing and borrowed from it.

Like other Reformation liturgists, Cranmer started
cautiously. His *Order for Communion* of 1548 presupposed
the continuance of the Latin rite, and though in that same
year he was in favour of an English rite, he was still in doubt
as to whether to prescribe the reading of the Canon in English
or Latin. However, in 1549 his first prayer book appeared
and was entirely in English. Its order was :

I.

Lord's Prayer (said by priest alone) and Collect for Purity—
   a remnant of the Latin preparation for the ministers.
Lord have mercy upon us (three times)
Glory be to God on high . . .
Salutation and Collect for the Day followed by two collects
      for the Sovereign
Epistle and Gospel
Nicene Creed
Sermon or printed homily, two of the latter being provided

II.

Offertory sentences (one or more), during which the people
   come up and put their money in a box, the communicants
   go forward to the choir or front of the church, and the
   minister prepares the elements
Salutation, *Sursum corda,* etc.
Preface (five Proper Prefaces being provided)
Sanctus
Eucharistic prayer :
(a) Intercession for the Church, including commemoration
    of the saints and prayer for the dead.
(b) Commemoration of redemption.

(c) A prayer of blessing and consecration.[1]

(d) Narrative of the Institution—a conflation of the biblical narratives.

(e) Anamnesis.

(f) Oblation ('of our self our souls and bodies . . .'), ending with a request to God to 'command these our prayers and supplications, by the ministry of thy holy angels, to be brought up into thy holy tabernacle before the sight of thy divine majesty, not weighing our merits, but pardoning our offences'. Note the close following of the language and figurative concepts of the Latin canon, but with the significant omission of all reference to sacrifice. The Lord's Prayer is then (with introductory sentence) said by the Priest. The people say : 'But deliver us from evil. Amen.'

The Peace.

'Christ our Paschal Lamb . . . ' A paraphrase of part of 1 Corinthians 5, 7, 8, echoing the proper preface for Easter.

The communion devotions (as in the *Order of Communion* 1548).

The communion of ministers followed by the people, during which the *Agnus Dei* is sung.

A post-communion sentence (for which a large choice is given) to be said or sung.

Salutation and Post-communion Collect.

Benediction, as in Roman rite.

The sterling quality of Cranmer's work is indicated by the fact that, though he was moved to produce a second edition of the Prayer Book in 1552 in which the Communion Service

---

[1] This is in the form of an invocation of the Holy Spirit which at one time led English liturgists to conjecture that Cranmer modelled it on the Eastern *Epiklesis,* in spite of the fact that it precedes rather than follows the Words of Institution. It is now, however, generally agreed that Cranmer, even if he had read some Eastern liturgies either in Greek or in a Latin translation, did not make use of them here or elsewhere. This particular prayer seems to have been compiled with the guidance of Latin sources.

was radically revised in a more Protestant direction, and in this revision several passages were cut out and the order of others changed, he was able to effect this revision with very few changes in the wording of the parts he retained. Moreover that wording has survived almost in its entirety to the present day. Some may attribute this to the conservatism of Anglicans and their stress on uniformity in worship; but Cranmer must be given his due.

At only one point is there a certain abruptness which amounts to faultiness of workmanship. The intercession which comes at the beginning of the eucharistic prayer connects neither with the Preface and *Sanctus* which precede it nor with the commemoration of redemption which follows. If, as seems probable, this prayer for the Church was derived from the Roman *Secrets* (offertory prayers) or the bidding prayers of *Prone,* or both, rather than from the intercessions of the Roman Canon, it may have been originally intended as an offertory prayer. In this case, either with the intention of soft-pedalling the offertory as in its sacrificial character contrary to Reformation principles, or to satisfy the conservatives who wished to retain intercessions within the Canon, it may have been transferred to this position at the last moment. To have what was essentially an offertory prayer after the *Sanctus* might not have been regarded as a very radical change if we take into account the fact that the Roman offertory in some measure anticipates the Canon and in the late Middle Ages came to be called the 'lesser canon'.

Another possible explanation is that there may have been a prayer of oblation (to which reference is made in a disputation of the time) in its Roman position immediately after the intercession, which would have formed the connecting link with the rest of the eucharistic prayer, and that this was removed at the last moment in accord with a desire to delete all reference to the sacrifice of the Mass.

Cranmer may well have intended his first Communion rite only as a transitional stage in his plan to produce one which

K

more fully embodied Reformation doctrine. In his Prayer Book of 1552 the most important changes are :

1. The replacement of the threefold *Kyrie* by the Decalogue (as in some continental rites with an expansion of the Kyrie as a response after each commandment). This (no doubt by a happy coincidence) provided the rite with at least a fixed Old Testament lection which had been largely lacking in liturgies since the fourth century.

2. The prayer for the Church was removed from the eucharistic prayer and placed after the offertory sentences. As we have seen, this may have been in Cranmer's original plan. Also no doubt by a happy coincidence, this was a return to a more primitive order. Cranmer is not likely to have known that the ancient great intercession for the Church which had disappeared from the Roman rite came approximately at this point. He was probably guided by Lutheran models of which we have discussed examples above. In any case this prayer is now only an offering of prayer.[1] The bread and wine are laid on the table either before the service begins or immediately before the consecration prayer, no specific direction about this being given. Even the money is no longer brought up by the people, but collected by the churchwardens, or those appointed by them, and placed in a box without being brought up to the holy table; so that to all intents and purposes the offertory has disappeared. References to the saints and the departed were also omitted.

3. A third homily is added. These homilies are seldom read now.

4. The Exhortation to confession, Confession, Absolution and Comfortable Words are placed before the *Sursum corda*. It may be said that this act with its emphasis on 'love and charity with your neighbours' takes the place of the Kiss of Peace in the ancient liturgies and is in the original position of

[1] Many of the Roman *secrets* specify offering of prayer as well as of the elements, this being a vestige of the original character of these prayers as collects in the great intercession.

that act. Another happy coincidence; but all that we have mentioned show Cranmer's sound liturgical sense in spite of the limitations in the knowledge of ancient rites which he shared with his contemporaries. Anglicans can, not without justice, claim that many of the improvements now thought desirable by the Roman liturgical movement were anticipated by Cranmer four centuries ago.

5. The transference of the Prayer of Humble Access to a position immediately before the eucharistic prayer. This was not so happy a change, but one necessitated by Cranmer's desire to have the Communion immediately after the Narrative of the Institution.

6. The most crucial change, concerning which controversy is still liable to burn within the Anglican Communion, was the radical revision of the eucharistic prayer in which (a) the prayer for the blessing of the Holy Spirit, and (b) the *Anamnesis* were omitted, and (c) the Communion of ministers and people was brought forward to a position immediately after the Narrative of the Institution, while (d) the prayer of self-offering (with the omission of several phrases and sentences) was placed after Communion with the post-communion prayer of thanksgiving left as an alternative to it.

Those who regret this change cannot charge Cranmer with ignorance or clumsiness. He knew what he was doing, and his new construction was a brilliant expression in liturgical form of the eucharistic doctrine which he held.[1] At the same time it is probably going too far to maintain, as do Dix and others, that the real meaning of the new rite lies in Cranmer's supposedly Zwinglian concept of the Eucharist, even if there is considerable evidence for his holding this view. He appears to have been statesman enough to realize the need for some measure of compromise. Also he steered clear of the error of the continental reformers of introducing didactic into liturgy.

---

[1] The revision was partly actuated by the attempt of English conservatives to interpret the 1549 eucharistic prayer in the sense of the Roman Canon.

Too precise a formulation of theology in the theological jargon of a period is bound to be 'dated' when the generation which formulated it has passed. The fact that Cranmer's liturgy is still used with acceptance shows that he avoided this.

Rather we must look for an interpretation of the English rite in the English Article of Religion (28) which repudiates the doctrine of transubstantiation on the one hand and an extreme Zwinglian doctrine on the other, but allows a considerable liberty of interpretation within these boundaries. It is the merit of the Anglican Prayer Book as a whole that its doctrinal expression is of this broad character.

Moreover it is a reasonable interpretation of the rite to regard this re-ordering of the eucharistic prayer as a most discerning expression in liturgical form of the nature of the eucharistic sacrifice as the self-sacrifice of the Church after its members have been united with Christ in his self-sacrifice, the emphasis being that this can only happen liturgically *after* the ministers and people have been united with Christ in communion. This is strangely close to the eucharistic teaching of some modern Roman Catholics, e.g., de la Taille and Jungmann (see above), though it does not altogether accord with Jungmann's contention that the sacrifice of Christ grows out of the offerings of the Church. Doubtless both Cranmer and these modern writers had meditated upon the eucharistic teaching of Augustine.

On the other hand, those who disapprove of Cranmer's placing of the oblation after Communion (and the partial following of his example in the *Order for the Lord's Supper* of the Church of South India) can point to the offertory in the early Church, whose members might well have said that they made the oblation of themselves when they brought up their gifts. God, they would say, has no need of our gifts, and yet, in a way beyond our understanding, joins them with the sacrifice of Christ and brings them to the 'heavenly altar'. After Communion our prayer should rather be, in the words of the Order for Holy Communion in the United Church of

Canada, that we may 'advance and grow in that faith which is effectual unto every good work'.

7. The *Gloria in excelsis* was transferred to the end of the service before the blessing as a post-communion act of adoration. It is magnificent here, as far as its first paragraph goes, but the penitential character of the second part leads one regretfully to admit that its right place is the traditional one near the beginning of the service; though even here it belongs to by no means the earliest stratum of the Western liturgy.

This rite of 1552, with a few later alterations (notably the restoration of an offertory, though one in a minor key) is substantially the rite known to Anglicans across the world both in English and in many translations—the rite of the *Book of Common Prayer* of 1662.[1] Though the 1549 rite was short-lived, its heritage has not been lost in the Anglican Communion. It was the basis for the Order of Holy Communion in the Prayer Book which was prepared for Scotland in 1637, but failed to receive acceptance. This later became substantially the rite of the small Episcopal Church in Scotland and of the Episcopal Church of America. It has been the chief model for modern revisions of the Anglican liturgy.

The 1662 Prayer Book has been the charter of Anglican 'evangelicals'[2] and the 1637 book the flag of the 'catholic'[2] party in the Anglican Communion. But 'evangelicals' who have pursued liturgical studies are now inclined to recognize at least the desirability of an *Anamnesis* in the eucharistic prayer, and there has developed considerable agreement between the

1 It is also substantially the rite of the British Methodists, at least those of the Wesleyan heritage. They prepare the elements before the service, as in the 1552 rite, and have a prayer for forgiveness instead of the declaratory absolution. They assert the corporateness of the act of Communion by communicating by 'tables', a practice which has been adopted by C.S.I. Methodists of the Primitive heritage prefer a rite close to that of the Congregationalists.

2 These adjectives are deliberately put in inverted commas as a mild protest against their being used as party labels. 'Catholics' presumably wish to be loyal to the *evangelium*, while 'evangelicals' regard themselves as loyal members of the *catholica ecclesia*.

two standpoints as to the nature of the eucharistic sacrifice; so that Anglican liturgical revision has a more hopeful outlook.

REVISION IN VARIOUS PROVINCES OF THE ANGLICAN COMMUNION

We need not delay over the abortive 1928 revision in England which satisfied few, perhaps because it was based on liturgical studies in a transitional period. Some elements in it of value—new collects and lections for holy days, a wider selection of proper prefaces, a revised Prayer for the Church which is in part a return to the 1549 prayer, as well as occasional intercessions to be used at Morning and Evening Prayer—have been accepted into the prayer books of more than one province of the Anglican Communion for some years now.

As an example of such revision which is of interest as combining Eastern and Western elements, mention may be made of the Order for the Lord's Supper in *The Book of Common Prayer* of the Church of India, Pakistan, Burma and Ceylon, which received final approval as the prayer book of this Anglican province in 1960.[1] The 1662 rite still remains in the prayer book as an alternative to the 1960 rite. Its preparation at this juncture when C.I.P.B.C. is committed to schemes of Church Union in India, Pakistan and Ceylon is presumably to put the Anglican liturgical heritage into acceptable order before taking it into union as a contribution to the united Churches.

Its main features as compared with the older rite, are :

1. A preparatory devotion of the minister and people (adapted from the Roman *Confiteor*).

2. Alternatives to the Decalogue : (*a*) Our Lord's summary of the Law or (*b*) the ninefold *Kyrie* (in the vernacular or in Greek as in the Syrian Churches).

3. An alternative to the continuous intercession for the Church in an offertory prayer followed by a litany of inter-

[1] Published by I.S.P.C.K. (Madras, Delhi, Lahore).

cession, which is largely the old prayer in litany form. At the conclusion of the litany the celebrant prays :

Hasten, O Father, the coming of thy kingdom; and grant that we and all thy servants, being quickened together in the eternal fellowship of thy Holy Spirit, may with joy behold thy Son at his coming again in glorious Majesty, even Jesus Christ, our only Mediator and Advocate.

And the people respond: Amen, come Lord Jesus.

There is a correspondence with the prayer 'Be present, be present . . .' which comes at a later point in the C.S.I. rite.

4. The eucharistic prayer echoes the *Liturgy of St. James* in the opening sentence. After the Words of Institution it has *Anamnesis,* Oblation and *Epiklesis,* the last in the C.S.I. form.

5. The Lord's Prayer with introductory sentence ('As our Saviour Christ hath commanded and taught us, we are bold to say :') is followed by the Peace in the Western position (this is optional) and the Prayer of Humble Access after silence (another C.S.I. feature). The *Agnus Dei* may be sung before communion. The Fraction has taken place in the traditional Anglican position during the Narrative of the Institution.

THE RITE OF THE CHURCH OF SOUTH INDIA

Comment in detail may be found elsewhere[1] on this Order for the Lord's Supper. Only an outline therefore is given here with a few observations appended.

A preparatory service to be held on the previous day or before the celebration. This may be composed at the discretion of the minister, though the reading of 1 Corinthians 11. 23-29, the Decalogue, our Lord's summary of the Law, and an exhortation, are suggested as suitable elements for inclusion in it.

Processional hymn with entrance of the ministers, one of them carrying the Bible.

Collect for purity.

Gloria in excelsis or *Trisagion* or a responsive reading from

[1] In T. S. Garrett, *The Liturgy of the Church of South India* and *Worship in the Church of South India.*

144 CHRISTIAN WORSHIP

Revelation ('the 'Litany of the Lamb') or a hymn.

Exhortation to self-examination, silence, exhortation to confession, confession, gracious words, declaration of forgiveness, response of the people.

Salutation, collect, Old Testament lection, Epistle, Gospel, Sermon, Creed (Nicene or Apostles').

Intercession for the Church, led by the deacon, either extempore or in one of two litany forms, the former being an adaptation of the Anglican intercession, the latter being derived from the *Liturgy of St. James;* one of two alternative concluding collects by the celebrant; the Pauline grace.

Offertory sentence and response; The Peace (given in the Syrian manner; see p. 78); offertory hymn, procession and prayer.

The prayer, 'Be present, be present...'—C.S.I.'s *Marana tha.*

Salutation, *Sursum corda,* etc.

Preface, with proper prefaces for certain days, *Sanctus, Benedictus qui venit* (in the Syrian form : 'he that hath come and is to come').

Eucharistic prayer (which includes commemoration of Incarnation and Redemption, Narrative of the Institution, *Anamnesis* with the two responses adapted from the *Liturgy of St. James, Epiklesis* which stresses communion rather than consecration and is therefore after the pattern of the pre-Nicene *Epiklesis.*

The Lord's Prayer with introductory sentence from the 1549 Prayer Book, silence, the Prayer of Humble Access, Fraction, Communion, during which the *Agnus Dei* or some other hymn may be sung. The Methodist practice of Communion by 'tables' is recommended, i.e., a whole row of communicants remaining kneeling till all have communicated, as a sign of the corporateness of the act.

The alternative post-communion prayers which may be said by all, one a new composition, the other derived from the Anglican post-communion prayers and both containing thanksgiving and self-offering in union with the self-offering of Christ. It is to be noted that this service adheres to Cranmer's placing of self-oblation after communion as theologically the right order. This is followed by a response of thanksgiving (Revelation 7. 12) said by all.

Blessing as in the Anglican rite.

As one who is wedded to this liturgy and would wish always to live by it, I would define its merits briefly as :

(a) The restoration of the classical pattern, while at the same time preserving the insights of the Reformation.

(b) The giving of full expression to the corporateness of the rite in the participation by the people throughout the rite in co-operation with the ministers. This is the ethos of primitive Christian worship, as we have seen in chapter 4. It has also been remarkably maintained by the Indian Christians of St. Thomas against all tendencies in the developed Eastern rites to the contrary. Is this India's specific contribution to the worship of the world-wide Church?

(c) An elasticity which allows for great variety, including extempore as well as liturgical prayer, as is right in a Church which has united various heritages. This also accords with the spirit of the fluid rite of the first four centuries.

Finally, without apology for repetition, we must say again that the fact that three independent liturgy committees in India supported by the higher councils of their Churches, the Lutheran, the Church of South India, and the Anglican, have all been led to restore the classical shape of the liturgy along much the same lines is an event or sequence of events which may be of untold importance for the future worship of the Church not only in India, but at least in other parts of Asia, It may also be a cogent factor in leading the Church to unity.

CHAPTER 8

ORDINATION[1]

ORDINATION may be considered here, as its proper time of performance is during the celebration of the Eucharist. The rite and those who receive it are thus incorporated in the central act of the Church's worship, and the newly ordained make their obedience to their call to the ministry part of their eucharistic offertory.

Let us preface our account of ordination with a cautionary tale about another rite. In a certain parish in England the minister-in-charge was in the habit of holding a 'vigil service' for his Confirmation candidates the night before each Confirmation and presenting them at it with a book and a flower. An imaginative and commendable practice, one might think; but a girl who had been confirmed in this parish, when asked what she had received at Confirmation, replied, 'A book and a flower'. The dramatic little outward ceremony which was intended to point to and prepare for the central act and its inward gift had ousted the latter in her imagination. Something like this has too often happened in the history of Ordination rites. Additional ceremonies, intended as subordinate symbolism, have tended to overshadow the central act of prayer with the laying on of hands which we find in Hippolytus and the early rites; prayer, that is, for the spiritual gift (Greek, *charisma*) for the work of the ministry to which the candidate has been called. This obscuring of the significance of the laying on of hands with prayer no doubt occurred first in the minds of the laity, for whom ceremonies such as

[1] For further details of the history of ordination read the chapter 'The Ordinal' by W. K. Firminger in *Liturgy and Worship*.

the putting on of priestly and episcopal garments, the anointing with oil, the presentation of the instruments of office, were more dramatic than the laying on of hands. But such misunderstanding eventually found its way into official pronouncements of the Church. The most striking example of this is the declaration by Pope Eugenius in the fourteenth century that the presentation of the chalice with wine and water and the paten with bread upon it to priests at their ordination (*porrectio instrumentorum*) with the words, 'Receive power to offer sacrifice to God and to celebrate Masses as well for the living as for the dead', was what made them priests. The omission of this ceremony from ordination services in the churches of the Reformation, e.g., the Anglican, is still officially regarded by Rome as a sign that the churches concerned do not intend to ordain sacrificing priests and that therefore their ordinations are 'invalid', though Roman Catholics admit that this ceremony (never adopted in the East) only found its way into Western ordinations in the Middle Ages. The point is that it is one thing for the Eastern Orthodox not to include a ceremony and its formula which have never been in their rites, but quite another for the reformers of the Western heritage to omit it. There are, however, signs that Roman theologians are not altogether satisfied with this position.

Another example of this kind of development is the second laying on of hands by the bishop in priest's Ordination in the Western church which in the Middle Ages (about the thirteenth century) was introduced at the end of the rite after Communion. The formula which accompanies it is:

Receive the Holy Spirit; whose sins thou shalt remit, they are remitted unto them; and whose sins thou shalt retain, they are retained.

There is a similar formula at an earlier point in the Roman deacon's Ordination. The purpose of this additional ceremony was similar to that of the *porrectio instrumentorum*, i.e., to make clear the intention of ordination by declaring a function of the priest's ministry, in this case the absolution of sins. It was not intended to supplement the original laying on of hands with prayer (in Rome the laying on of hands being performed silently before the Ordination Prayer). By the time of the Reformation, however, it had been forgotten that this was a late addition to the rite.

Cranmer was evidently deceived by the biblical character of the formula (John 20. 22, 23) into thinking that *this* was the primitive apostolic act of Ordination. He therefore omitted the laying on of hands before the Ordination Prayer and made this secondary laying on of hands the only one, adapting it to fit each order of the ministry and bringing it forward to a position immediately after the Ordination Prayer, and in deacon's Ordination omitting the ordination prayer altogether. Whereas for the original laying on of hands and Ordination Prayer the Bishop stands as a father-in-God praying for his sons in the Gospel, for the subsidiary ceremonies—vesting, anointing, *porrectio instrumentorum* and this final laying on of hands—he sits after the manner of a magistrate conferring insignia of office on his subordinates, and this latter posture has been adopted for the formula of Ordination by Anglican bishops. This tends to obscure the truth, which all would admit, that it is God who ordains.

Though the Eastern Churches have better maintained the centrality of the Ordination Prayer with its accompanying laying on of hands, there is a tendency among Eastern Orthodox theologians to regard as the essential 'form' of Ordination the proclamation made before the Ordination Prayer :

> The divine grace which always healeth that which is sick and filleth up that which is lacking advances [N.] the most pious deacon to presbyter. Let us all therefore pray for him that the grace of the All-Holy Spirit may come upon him.

This is said by the bishop as he lays his hands on the head of the candidate and he continues to lay on his hands while saying two ordination prayers secretly.

In the Syrian Churches of India there is some elaboration
of ceremony intended to symbolize the imparting of the holiness of the altar and the sacrament of life which lies upon it to
the ordained. After the Ordination Prayer, the bishop lays his
right hand on the head of the candidate and says :

Thou art ordained in the Holy Church of God.[1]

We note here too the overshadowing of the central act by
subsidiary ceremonies. In the consecration of bishops, for
instance, there is a tendency to regard the presentation of the
pastoral staff to the newly consecrated bishop by his conse-
crators as the act which makes him a bishop.

Important revisions of the Ordinal have taken place in
India recently, namely *The Ordinal* of the Church of South
India and the proposed ordination services for the future
united Churches of North India and Pakistan.[2] These latter
services are at present printed only in *The Proposed Services
for the Inauguration of the Churches of North India and
Pakistan*. The two ordinals are substantially the same, as
North and South India worked in close co-operation. In them
the central act of prayer with laying on of hands is given its
proper place. Tribute must be paid to the previous work of
liturgists of the Church of Scotland in the ordination rite of
The Ordinal and Service Book upon which these revised
Indian rites are largely based. Indeed those non-episcopal
churches which have retained ordination by the laying on of
hands by the presbytery have in general preserved the primitive form of the Ordination Prayer with its accompanying
laying on of hands better than the ordination rites of the
episcopal churches.

[1] For further details see L. W. Brown, *The Indian Christians of St.
Thomas*, pp. 264-74.

[2] See E. C. Ratcliff, 'The Ordinal of the Church of South India' in *Theology*,
January 1960, and T. S. Garrett in *Scottish Journal of Theology*, December
1959.

CHAPTER 9

THE CONSECRATION OF LIFE

THE central act of the Church's worship which we have been studying in the preceding chapters symbolizes in the offering of bread and wine and its setting apart for sacramental use the consecration of man's daily life in the service of God. But Christian piety has from early times extended this sanctification of life in (a) a daily cycle of prayer, and (b) an annual cycle of holy days. Thus nature's time in the full round of Christian devotion becomes God's time. (c) This dedication of our creaturely existence to him is further signified in the occasional services which mark the events of human life : the solemnization of marriage, thanksgiving for childbirth, the visitation of the sick, the burial of the dead, the blessing of a house, the dedication of a church, intercessions for agriculture and other activities of man, the harvest thanksgiving.

Forms of service in this last category are too numerous and varied to be surveyed within the compass of this book. The student of them must be referred to the service books of the various Churches. We shall confine our study to the first two sections, i.e., the daily cycle of prayer and the calendar.

THE DAILY CYCLE OF PRAYER

We have already noted (in chapter 2) that the early Christians followed Jewish practice in praying at certain hours of the day. In Acts the apostles are recorded as praying at the third, sixth and ninth hours (9 a.m., 12 noon and 3 p.m.). There are numerous references to these hours of prayer in the writings of the Fathers, as well as to morning and evening prayers. In the case of the latter, connexion with the Jewish practice is demonstrated by the fact that Psalms 148, 149, 150, said at Lauds (see below) both in the East and the West, were recited at dawn by pious Jews in the first century, and the Eastern Orthodox still sing at Vespers (Evening Prayer) the hymn *Phōs hilaron* ('Hail gladdening light' in the well-known English translation), an early Christian hymn, composed for family prayer at the lighting of the lamp, a ceremony which Christians took over from Judaism.

FROM PRIVATE TO PUBLIC PRAYER

Until the fourth century there is no evidence for any public services at these hours of prayer. In times of persecution Christians would hardly risk coming together except for the vital celebration of the Eucharist. We may presume, therefore, that these hours of prayer were observed by individuals or at the most single households. They show us a Church whose faith and witness to the point of martyrdom were based on a disciplined life of personal devotion. This was also, as it ever should be, the solid foundation for the public worship of the Eucharist. Let those Churches today whose position in a non-Christian environment is so similar to that of the Church of the early centuries remember that their primitive counterpart triumphed by its rule of prayer.

The history of the transformation of this cycle of private prayer into a cycle of public worship (called the 'Choir Offices', or the 'Offices of the Hours', or, as a whole, the 'Daily Office') is by no means certain. In the *Apostolic Tradition* of Hippolytus (written in Rome early in the third century, see chapter 4) every Christian, whether minister, layman or laywoman, is commanded to pray on rising in the morning, at the third, sixth and ninth hours (which are now associated with the crucifixion), and on retiring to bed and at midnight, on account of our Lord's words concerning the bridegroom

coming at that hour. There is as yet no prayer at sunset, but
directions are given for a corporate supper at which the little
ceremony of the *lucernarium* (blessing of the lamp) takes
place, the bishop saying a thanksgiving very similar to 'Hail
gladdening light', which, as we have noted, later became a
part of Greek Vespers. There are also daily assemblies for
instruction, and the reading of the Scriptures at home is prescribed when public instruction is impossible.

All this is still private or domestic prayer, and there is no
trace of a corporate saying of 'offices'. One might argue that
such ecclesiastical regulation of private prayer was the first
step towards making it public. We must remember, however,
that Hippolytus was probably the leader of only one section
of the Church in Rome and may have imposed upon his
followers a stricter discpline than that which prevailed elsewhere. In any case, these hours of prayer in their entirety
could only have been observed by people of some leisure with
slaves to work for them, hardly by Christian slaves themselves.
Yet the laity who had the time to do so did undoubtedly go on
observing these hours of prayer and may often have observed
them together in houses, if not in churches. It was not until
after the conversion and victory of Constantine, which meant
the end of persecution and led to a great increase in the
building of churches, that public services at these hours could
begin to spread in the Church as a whole.

At this time another factor of importance in the development of this mode of worship comes into our picture, the great
spread of the monastic movement during the fourth century.
The monks adopted and added to these hours of prayer which
were already established among the 'secular' clergy and the
laity. The pioneers of this movement, the fathers of the
desert, lived solitary lives devoted to prayer and only met
occasionally for common worship; but when ascetics came to
be organized in religious communities, it was natural that
corporate services should be prescribed for them at intervals
throughout the day and night as part of their rule of life. An

early example of this is the *Longer Rule* which Basil the Great
prepared for the ascetics of Pontus and Cappadocia. This
scheme includes eight offices, i.e., at midnight, before the
dawn, at dawn, at the third, sixth and ninth hours, at evening
and at the beginning of the night. John Cassian in his
Institutes of the Coenobites describes the ascetics of Palestine
as observing seven hours of prayer. He regards this as a fulfilment of the Psalmist's promise, 'Seven times a day will I
praise thee.'

Evidently by the last quarter of the fourth century these
services were conducted publicly in the churches of Syria and
Palestine, if not as yet elsewhere. In the *Apostolic Constitutions* (see p. 59) there are two main services prescribed at
morning and evening and the offices of the lesser hours are
also said in church. The evidence of this and of John Cassian
is confirmed by the diary of Etheria, a Spanish lady, which
she kept on her pilgrimage to Palestine probably from 393 to
396 (*Peregrinatio Etheriae*). We learn from her account that
the morning service and the evening *lucernarium*[1] were particularly well attended by both laity and ascetics. We shall have
occasion to refer again to the important evidence of this
document for the development of the Calendar. Jerusalem,
as a place of pilgrimage in which there must have been a
demand for public services among the pilgrims, no doubt led
Christendom in this development, and pilgrims returning
home may well have spread the ways of worship in use there
by advocating their adoption in their own churches.

The Church in Rome with its usual conservatism was late in
introducing the cycle of public offices, but had evidently done
so by the beginning of the sixth century, when Benedict, the
father of Western monasticism, produced his *Rule* (about 530).
At this time Rome had six services : Vigil or Mattins, Lauds,
Terce, Sext, None and Vespers; Terce, Sext and None being
said only on Sundays and some holy days. Benedict prescribed

---

[1] i.e. Lauds and Vespers, as they were later called. These two services
may have become public ones at an early date in the cities.

L

for his monks the daily recitation of these three services, as well as of the others, and, probably following Basil, added Prime (the dawn office) and Compline (*completorium* = the completion of the day). He also introduced the hymns of St. Ambrose (or hymns composed in his manner) to be sung at these services. This was the foundation of the monastic Breviary (book of offices). During the Middle Ages it considerably influenced the secular Breviary from which it had been derived; so that the new services introduced by the monks were taken over from it.

The original Roman scheme included the ordered reading of the Bible, and the recitation of the Psalter during the course of a week. It was fundamentally biblical in character and gave to the Church a disciplined knowledge of the Bible. But during the Middle Ages confusions and complications set in with the introduction of special offices for the holy days which were at first observed as 'doubles' (i.e., offices said in addition to the regular ones) and then tended to supersede them. With the introduction by the Franciscans (whose Breviary prevailed throughout the West from the thirteenth century onwards) of special offices not only for a holy day itself, but for the seven days which followed it also, and with the increasing number of Saints' days, the old ferial (ordinary) office fell largely into disuse and the offices became a succession of festal observances. Another regrettable innovation was the introduction of readings from the more or less mythical lives of saints. Other accretions to the daily cycle were the votive offices of the Virgin Mary and of the Dead which in England were translated into English in the *Prymer* and became, along with other devotional material in the *Prymer,* the normal liturgical prayer of the pious laity. The older offices, which were only in Latin, came to be regarded mainly as the concern of the clergy. A further stultification of the original scheme was the practice which grew up among the secular clergy in the latter part of the Middle Ages of saying the offices, not at their appointed hours, but one after another in two or three groups, a usage

which involved much vain repetition, as well as rendering
meaningless those passages in the offices which referred to the
particular hour of the day.[1]

MORNING AND EVENING PRAYER IN THE REFORMED CHURCHES

By the end of the Middle Ages the Breviary clearly needed
reform and attempts were made at this in the Western Church,
the most notable being that of Cardinal Quiñones, published
in 1535, which aimed at simplification and the restoration of
the ordered reading of the Psalter and other books of the
Bible. Though this revision was opposed as too radical by
the Roman hierarchy and was eventually suppressed, it prepared the way for the Breviary of Pope Pius V (1568) which
together with his Missal of two years later established uniformity in the Roman Church. Quiñones' Breviary also influenced
the work of the reformers, in particular that of Cranmer.

[1] For further details see essays in *Liturgy and Worship,* especially
E. C. Ratcliff's essay, 'The Choir Offices'. R. French's essay, 'The
Services of the Eastern Orthodox Church', in the same volume has
an account of the Eastern Orthodox Offices. These too are now
recited in groups. A distinctive feature of them is the *troparia*
which are linked together with *glorias* and quotations from the
Psalms to form a garland of worship. A *troparion* is a composition
in poetic language, though not in metre. A well-known example is
the *phōs hilaron* (see above). The *gloria in excelsis* is a composition
of the same character.

For the offices of the Syrian Christians in India see L. W. Brown,
The Indian Christians of St. Thomas, ch. ix. They too recite their
seven offices in two groups, three in the early morning and the other
four about sunset. Each office begins with the *Kauma* (*Sanctus* and
expansion of the *Trisagion,* see p. 81) and Lord's Prayer and ends
with the *Kauma* and the Creed, though the Creed is only said once
when the offices are grouped together. The offices include an
ordered reading of the Psalms, the *ekbo* (a short collect), *Stoumen
kalōs* (let us stand well), *Kyrie eleison,* the prayer of incense, prayers
to the Mother of God, the saints, a prayer of contrition and one for
the dead. There are also hymns for the different days of the week
in every season.

The Church of South India has introduced the *Kauma* as an
initial act of adoration (though only for optional use) in its *Order
for Morning and Evening Prayer.*

The reformers, however, were not content with what they could only regard as half measures. While in other Churches of the Reformation the daily office was abolished in favour of more informal ways of worship, the Lutherans and Cranmer, who was much influenced by them, included in their service books orders for Mattins and Vespers or Evensong (Morning and Evening Prayer). For Mattins Cranmer may have followed the morning service for Sundays and holy days in the Lutheran Church Order of Calenberg-Göttingen; for both services have a similar structure and combine the old old services of Mattins and Lauds. But while the Lutheran Order for Vespers closely follows the Breviary service, Cranmer's Evensong is a combination of the old Vespers and Compline. It is perhaps Cranmer's best liturgical composition and in its ordered sequence is a model for this type of worship.[1]

In the first English Prayer Book of 1549 Mattins and Evensong are very brief services, beginning with the Lord's Prayer and ending with the three Collects. They were evidently intended as forms of daily prayer which on Sundays and holy days would be subordinate to the Holy Communion, the latter being the main service of the day. But in 1552 an exhortation, confession and absolution were added at the beginning and the Litany was to be used on Sundays, Wednesdays and Fridays and at such other times as the bishop ordained. In 1662 an anthem, four collects, a general thanksgiving, other prayers, and the grace were added at the end. To this common custom has added a sermon and hymns.

This was no doubt done because of the immediate popular preference for these services. The reformers in England and elsewhere were unable to establish Holy Communion as the normal Sunday service. In most parishes it was celebrated only rarely; though in recent years the anglo-catholic liturgical

[1] Orders for Prime and Compline are found in the 1928 *Book of Common Prayer* and Compline at least in other modern revisions of the Anglican Prayer Book.

revival has in some measure redressed the balance even in congregations which would not call themselves 'anglo-catholic', as also has the less widespread liturgical revival in the Lutheran Churches. In other protestant Churches there has been the development of Sunday orders of worship not unlike Morning and Evening Prayer in general plan, but more elastic in structure and giving place to extempore rather than liturgical prayer. As in the Anglican form, the sermon tends unfortunately to be separated from the act of worship. It should come after the lessons, as in the C.S.I. Morning and Evening Prayer, rather than at the end of the service, and so be brought into conjunction with the reading of the Word of God.

ANTE-COMMUNION AND MORNING PRAYER

But another form of Sunday worship must also be noted. In the majority of Lutheran congregations, as well as in many other Churches of the Reformation, the normal Sunday morning service, when there is no Communion, is the Ante-Communion, i.e., the first part of the eucharistic liturgy which corresponds to the ancient Liturgy of the Catechumens. In Anglican churches too the Ante-Communion may be read after Morning Prayer when there is no Communion. So too the Church of South India has recommended the use of this part of its liturgy as the main Sunday service when there is no celebration of the Lord's Supper.

As we have seen in our study of the early history of the eucharistic liturgy, this first part of the rite probably developed from the worship of the synagogue which the primitive Church adopted and at an early date made integral with the celebration of the Eucharist. It belonged essentially to the *synaxis* or meeting of the *ecclesia* in each locality for eucharistic worship. The origin and history of Morning and Evening Prayer, whether of the liturgical or 'free' variety, is different. Though they too have a Jewish origin, they began as the private devotions of ministers and laity. These, as the daily office, became popular public services for a short period from the fourth century onwards, but soon were left to the religious orders and secular clergy as their concern, with only rare attendance by the laity. The reformers restored these services in a simplified form to the people, and it is a fact of modern Church history which we must accept that they have largely become the main way of worship on the Lord's Day.

THE YOUNGER CHURCHES

In the protestant Churches of Asia and Africa there is, alas, on the average only one ordained minister to fifteen congregations or more.[1] Until *either* the Churches have more resources to support more ministers, *or* (and this may be the more realistic approach) they take bolder steps to train and ordain a voluntary ministry in every congregation, the celebration of the Lord's Supper in every congregation on every Lord's Day must remain a remote ideal. The choice on a Sunday morning lies between Ante-Communion and Morning Prayer in one of its many forms. Though the history of these services is very different and their diverse origin is plain in their differences of structure, their content and general purpose as acts of worship is surprisingly the same. It is, as the Anglican exhortation to confession at Morning and Evening Prayer puts it, 'to render thanks for the great benefits that we have received at his [God's] hands, to set forth his most worthy praise, to hear his most holy Word, and to ask those things which are requisite and necessary as well for the body as the soul'. Those who have the responsibility of conducting public worship in congregations where some freedom of order is allowed would do well to remember these words as stating the elements essential to a full act of public worship, i.e., together with confession and declaration of forgiveness, which is the subject of this exhortation, must go adoration and thanks-

[1] See Lincoln Watts, *What the Figures Tell* (World Dominion Press, 1950).

giving, the reading and preaching of the Word of God, and intercession for the Church and the World. These are the elements common to both Ante-Communion and Morning and Evening Prayer. We may also venture to say that, though the former has a longer history of corporate use as the Sunday service of the congregation, the latter has greater elasticity and adaptability, and no congregation need be censured for preferring it. Indeed it might be argued that Ante-Communion without Communion (except perhaps on Good Friday and Easter Eve when there is a special reason for it) is like a royal procession without the king, and that if Communion is not celebrated, it would be better not to have it. This seems to be the view of Dr. C. H. Swavely, a Lutheran missionary in India, who presumably represents a section of Lutheran opinion when he writes, 'Whenever there is no Communion the proper service to be used is Matins in the morning and Vespers in the evening.'[1] In this, however, he differs from the rubrics of the *Common Service Book of the Lutheran Church*.

Some protestant Churches have evolved the custom of celebrating Holy Communion in a very brief rite after their particular form of Morning or Evening Prayer. This is deplored by liturgical purists, largely because in the way in which it is often done it seems to relegate the Eucharist to the position of an optional extra to the main act of congregational worship, as well as truncating the rite. Those who follow this usage should bear this criticism in mind; but they might well defend themselves by pointing out that if the content and purpose of the Ante-Communion and of Morning and Evening Prayer are so much the same as to make it possible to regard them as equivalents, the fault is not perhaps after all such a heinous one, particularly if Morning or Evening Prayer has been so ordered as to make it a preparation for Communion. In any case, they might argue, this mode of celebrating Holy Communion is less objectionable than that of celebrating the complete rite without a sermon and with only fragmentary

1 *Worship in the Lutheran Church* (Guntur, India), p. 19.

readings from the Bible. The importance of the dominant position which Morning and Evening Prayer have taken in the worship of Protestant Churches is that they assert that Holy Communion can only have its proper place in the Church's life and be rightly understood if it is set in the context of a Ministry of the Word which is on an equal footing with the Ministry of the Sacraments.

THE CALENDAR[1]

SUNDAY

We learn from the New Testament[2] that the primitive Church met for worship on the first day of the week and that from early times this was called 'the Lord's Day'.[3] There is perhaps no more convincing witness to the resurrection than this transference of the Church's worship from Saturday (the Jewish Sabbath) to Sunday. Indeed every Sunday is a little Easter, with its eucharistic showing forth of Christ's death and resurrection and its eschatological hope of the coming of his kingdom. The Seventh Day Adventists who advocate a return to the observance of Saturday as the Sabbath have completely failed to understand the significance of Sunday.

THE CHRISTIAN PASCHA

One season of the year supremely combined this historical remembrance and transcendent hope, the Jewish festival of the *Pascha* during which the passion and the resurrection took place. This is undoubtedly the most primitive festival of the Christian year. Paul may well be referring to it in 1 Corinthians 5. 7-8 when he writes : 'Christ, our paschal Lamb, has been sacrificed. Let us, therefore, celebrate the festival . . .' and 1 Peter may well be a sermon for this feast. In the latter part

---

[1] See: A. A. McArthur, *The Evolution of the Christian Year*; G. Dix, *The Shape of the Liturgy*, ch. xi; O. Cullmann, *The Early Church*, ch. ii; J. A. Jungmann, *Public Worship*, ch. ix.

[2] Acts 20. 7, 1 Cor. 16. 2.   [3] Rev. 1. 10.

of the second century there was some controversy as to when it should be celebrated. The orthodox churches of Asia (Asia Minor) observed it on the night of the 14th Nisan, i.e., according to Jewish lunar reckoning, regardless of the day of the week on which this fell; hence the name 'Quartodeciman'. This, according to the chronology of the Fourth Gospel, was the night of the Last Supper, Christ being crucified the following day (still the 14th Nisan which began in the evening), the day on which the paschal lambs were slain. Though the Asian Churches claimed that their tradition went back to to the apostolic period, it is probable that it arose as a result of the influence of the Fourth Gospel in Asia. The rest of the Church followed the doubtless more primitive tradition of observing the Christian *Pascha* on the first day of the week, the Sunday after the Jewish *Pascha,* reckoning it in Jewish fashion as beginning on the Saturday evening. In the third century the Asian Churches too conformed to this practice. While their practice laid stress on the crucifixion and that of the rest of the Church on the resurrection, it seems evident, as we shall see below, that the primitive *Pascha* combined commemoration of both the passion and the resurrection in a single festival.

There are a number of references to the *Pascha* in early Christian writings and we learn details of its observance in particular from the early Church orders, viz., *The Apostolic Tradition of Hippolytus* (Rome, early third century, but probably representing earlier usage), the *Didascalia Apostolorum* (Syria or Palestine, third century), and *The Testament of our Lord* (Asia Minor or Syria, mid fourth century); also from references in Tertullian's writings (North Africa, late second and third century).

From this evidence we learn that the *Pascha* was preceded by a two-day fast (*Apostolic Tradition*), which was later extended to a fast from Monday to Saturday in Holy Week, though with more rigorous fasting on the last two days. Eusebius in his *History of the Church* records that a fast of forty hours before Easter commemorated our Lord's forty hours in the tomb. The fast on the Friday was regarded by Hippolytus as less important than that on the Saturday, and the sick were excused from it. It is surprising thus to learn that before the latter half of the fourth century the Church no-where observed Good Friday as the commemoration of the crucifixion in distinction from Easter as the commemoration of the resurrection. The *Pascha* was a unitive festival showing forth our salvation in both events.

The great paschal Vigil—the 'mother of all vigils', as St. Augustine called it—began on the Saturday evening with a long series of lections, instruction and exorcism. Baptism (as we have described it in chapter 2) followed in some places before midnight (*Testament of our Lord*), in others at cock-crow (*Apostolic Tradition* and *Didascalia*). The joyous cele-bration of the Easter Eucharist, with the newly baptized receiving Communion for the first time along with the rest of the faithful, completed the paschal observance.

The ancient churches of East and West (and in recent times many Anglican congregations) have in large measure preserved this primitive tradition in their observance of the paschal Vigil. In the Roman Church this begins with the lighting of the paschal candle after all other lights have been extinguished. This glad symbol of the resurrection is kept lit at all services throughout the season of Easter. Then follows the order for Baptism, with a series of lections (chosen from the Old Testament for their typology of Baptism and Redemption) and collects, culminating in the renewal of their baptismal vows by the whole congregation. Finally comes the Vigil Mass (for many centuries displaced to Saturday morning, but lately restored by papal authority to its proper position), which is regarded as the first Mass of Easter. The order for this Mass is the most ancient in character of the whole Christian year, a signal instance of the 'liturgical law' we have already noted : 'the preservation of what is ancient in a season liturgically of high value'. Not all that Rome and the Eastern

Churches do on this night will be acceptable to Protestants; but a plea might reasonably be made for the restoration throughout Christendom of this most ancient—indeed probably apostolic—vigil. In passing we might observe that the annual renewal by the whole Church of our baptismal promises, in a baptismal service (without Baptism) read immediately before the Easter Eucharist, could go far to meet the difficulties of Baptists in uniting with those who practise infant Baptism.

HOLY WEEK AND GOOD FRIDAY

We have seen that the pre-Nicene Church only observed the *Pascha* during the night which ended on Easter Sunday morning with a fast of two days, later extended to six days, preceding, but with no other commemorations or observances marking the days of Holy Week. How then did the later liturgical development of Holy Week arise?

One factor was the observance from the second century onwards of 'stations', i.e., half-fasts until 3 p.m., on Wednesdays and Fridays. This may have been partly in imitation of the Jewish fasts on Mondays and Thursdays. The Church desired to distinguish itself from Judaism by choosing different days, but also chose these particular days as commemorating the betrayal and crucifixion of Jesus. These fasts at first were matters of private devotion rather than of general obligation; but, combined with the fact that the Friday before Easter was part of the pre-paschal fast, they paved the way for marking out that Friday as a day for particular remembrance of the crucifixion.

In tracing this development the document of paramount importance is the diary of Etheria recording her pilgrimage to Palestine which we have already had occasion to mention (see p. 153). Etheria tells of a magnificent round of liturgical observances during Holy Week (as also of other commemorations during the year), including a procession of palms on the Sunday before Easter, a great celebration of the Eucharist on

the evening of Maundy Thursday, and the veneration of the
cross and a service of lections and prayers concerning the
passion from noon to 3 p.m. on Good Friday. The catechetical
lectures of Cyril delivered in Jerusalem in 348, when he was
still a presbyter, give no evidence that these observances were
current at that time, nor is there any indication of any similar
commemorations elsewhere in the Church. We may therefore
conclude that they arose in Jerusalem itself during the inter-
vening period (348-393). After the Church had gained its
freedom with the victory of Constantine, there had been great
activity in identifying the holy places of Palestine connected
with the events of the Gospels, and Constantine himself had
led the way in building churches upon them. Pilgrims came in
large numbers, including many ascetics, to visit them. It was
natural therefore to provide, particularly in the Holy City and
in Bethlehem, liturgical commemorations at each holy place on
the particular day with which it was associated. Thus Jerusalem led the way in the development of a liturgical year the
basic structure of which was the events of the life of our Lord.
From what we know of Cyril, it is not unreasonable to conjecture that he was the creative genius who organized this
development during his episcopate. As with the daily office,
the pilgrims returning to their homes would be agents in
spreading the new tradition as that of the birth-place of
Christianity.

ASCENSION AND PENTECOST

The day which rabbinical Judaism associated with the giving
of the Law was for the Church the day of the outpouring of
the Spirit under the New Covenant. It is possible that Paul in
his contrast between the Law and the Spirit[1] had in mind the
difference between the Jewish Pentecost and the Christian.
We may reckon then at least with the possibility that its
observance in the Church goes back to apostolic times. The

[1] 2 Cor. 3. 3-8, Rom. 7. 6, 8. 2.

first definite evidence, however, comes from the third century in the writings of Tertullian, Hippolytus and Origen. By then it is well established. Tertullian speaks of the season from Easter to Whitsunday as the 'period of Pentecost'. During these fifty days Christians were forbidden to fast or to pray kneeling, a prohibition which applied to every Sunday. Thus they symbolized the joy and triumph of the resurrection.

Whitsunday was an appropriate occasion on which to baptize any who had missed Baptism at Easter. It is evident also from early references to it that, like the *Pascha*, it was a unitive festival comprising commemoration of the Ascension as well as the gift of the Spirit and the hope of Christ's coming of which the Spirit was the *arrabōn*[1] or guarantee. The Ascension, however, came eventually to be separated from Pentecost. Etheria's diary mentions a service at Bethlehem (not Jerusalem) on the fortieth day after Easter with sermons 'treating of things suitable to the day and place'. But this, as we learn from an ancient Armenian lectionary derived from Jerusalem, was evidently not the feast of the Ascension, but a commemoration of the children slain by Herod. In this case not Jerusalem but some other centre, perhaps Constantinople or Antioch, where the Ascension was observed as a separate festival before the end of the fourth century, led the way, and Jerusalem only followed other churches in the separation of the commemoration of the Ascension from Pentecost itself in the eighth or ninth century.[2] In this separation as well as in that of the commemoration of the Passion in distinction from the resurrection, we may discern a shift of emphasis from the supra-historical realities of salvation, life in the Spirit and the hope of the Age to Come, to the historical aspect of revelation in Christ. The beginnings of this change go back to the second century; but the new outlook was consonant with the changed

[1] *arrabōn* is the Greek word translated 'earnest' in 2 Cor. 1. 22 and Eph. 1. 14.

[2] For the evidence see McArthur, *Evolution of the Christian Year*, pp. 152ff.

position of the Church from the fourth century onwards, when it became an established historical institution and part of the structure of human society.

CHRISTMAS AND EPIPHANY

The date of the birth of Jesus is unknown. If we follow the account in Luke of shepherds staying out in the fields all night with their flocks it is unlikely that it took place in mid-winter. The traditional commemoration of the Nativity must therefore have been dated by other considerations.

Just as we are surprised, and perhaps shocked, to discover that there was no Good Friday before the latter half of the fourth century, so too we may be astonished to learn that Christmas was absent from the calendar of the early Church. This does not mean that there was no commemoration of the birth of Christ; for the Epiphany, a much older festival than Christmas, was originally, like the *Pascha* and Pentecost, a unitive festival. It commemorated the revelation of God to man both in the Incarnation and in the Baptism of Christ. Though the evidence for its general observance comes only from the fourth century, there are indications that it was observed much earlier, at least in some localities in the East. In particular there is a fragment of a sermon from the second century, found at the end of the *Epistle to Diognetus,* which can best be interpreted as connected with the Epiphany.[1] The reason for its dating on 6 January was probably that this was the traditional date of the winter solstice according to a very ancient calendar. Though this calendar was obsolete by the beginning of the Christian era, pagans still celebrated a festival of the birth of the sun-god on this date, and the Church may have wished to provide a Christian equivalent for the festival of the birth of light. It is

---

[1] *Epistle to Diognetus,* xi. 3, 4 : 'For this cause he sent forth the Word that he might be revealed in the world . . . This is he who is eternal and who today is reckoned Son, through whom the Church is enriched and grace is spread forth and abounds among the saints.'

interesting and perhaps significant, in view of the fact that the miracle of Cana has traditionally been connected with the season of Epiphany as an instance of the manifestation of Christ's divine power, to note that in Greece and Asia Minor a festival of Dionysus, the god of wine, was also celebrated on this date, with a myth of the god changing water into wine. It is too speculative a conjecture to suppose that the Prologue of St. John's Gospel and the account of the miracle of Cana were written with the Epiphany in mind.

It is uncertain whether the Church in Rome observed Epiphany before the fourth century. It is here that the observance of 25 December as the Feast of the Nativity is attested in the year 336 in the *Chronography* of Philocalus. A possible factor in the choosing of this date may have been the statement, found in the *Commentary on Daniel* of Hippolytus, that Jesus was born on 25 December and died on 25th March. The latter date, as the spring equinox, was regarded as the time of Creation, and the notion may have been that our Lord's life must have been a perfect period and that his conception took place on the same date as his death, which would place his birth nine months later. But Hippolytus had been dead for more than a century and his influence in Rome was negligible. A more likely reason for the choice of this date was the fact that since the time of the Emperor Aurelian 25 December, as the winter solstice, had been the festival of the Birth of the 'unconquerable sun' (*Sol Invictus*). If this be so, the influence of the emperor Constantine who had at his conversion tended to identify Christ with the unconquerable sun may have been exerted in this choice of date. Clearly Christians at the end of the fourth and the beginning of the fifth centuries were not unaware of the pagan festival. Ambrose in a sermon contrasts it with the Christian festival and declares that 'Christ is the new sun'. Similar references were made by Augustine and Leo.

In the general exchange of holy days between East and West the new festival was adopted by Constantinople in 379 and had been established throughout the East before the fifth century had advanced very far. This led to the transference of the commemoration of the birth of Christ from the Epiphany to Christmas, Epiphany in the East retaining only the commemoration of his Baptism. Rome, which, as we have seen, may have accepted the Epiphany as a festival at a late date, regarded it as the commemoration only of the visit of the Wise Men. This had doubtless been one element in the ancient unitive festival of the East. Though in North Italy, Gaul and Spain (see the Mozarabic collect for the Epiphany, p. 88) remembrance of Christ's Baptism continued for a time, the Roman tradition eventually prevailed in the West to the impoverishment of the meaning of the festival. In India the Eastern tradition has naturally been preserved in the Syrian Church (cf. the *Kauma* for Epiphany, 'O thou who wast baptized for us, have mercy upon us') and the lectionary of the Church of South India has reintroduced remembrance of the Baptism into the Epiphany season.

With the date of the Nativity thus fixed, it was not difficult to assign dates to other historical events in the Gospels, the Circumcision, the Presentation of Christ in the Temple, the Annunciation, etc. The inauguration of these holy days was the work of succeeding centuries. In the Middle Ages feasts connected with the Virgin Mary became particularly popular; but it is significant that none of them was generally established before the seventh century. The fortieth day after Christmas is mentioned by Etheria, as observed in Jerusalem. In the East today it is called Hypapante (= The Meeting), i.e., the day of the presentation of Christ in the Temple. In ancient Rome 1 January (now the Feast of the Circumcision) was observed as the birthday of Mary.

OTHER SEASONS AND FASTS

Advent. There is evidence of the observance in Spain of a period of three weeks preparatory to Epiphany in the fourth century. Evidently about the fifth century the six weeks before Christmas were observed in Gaul as a penitentiary period of preparation for Christmas. After a period of some variety in use, the Roman custom of observing an Advent of four Sundays prevailed.

Lent. We have already noted the 'stations' or half-fasts on Wednesdays and Fridays. In the fourth century, and possibly earlier, vigils were observed on Saturday nights and on the eves of Saints' days, possibly in imitation of the great paschal vigil.

The great fast of Lent which was established in the latter part of the fourth century had its antecedents in the earlier fast of candidates in preparation for Baptism. Its purpose was both to prepare for Easter and to commemorate our Lord's fasting in the wilderness, the latter being secondary to the former. At first it varied in length in different places. Etheria, who may have been used to a six-week fast in Spain, was evidently surprised to find an eight-week fast observed in Jerusalem. Finally the Roman custom prevailed of beginning Lent on Ash Wednesday, the fortieth day before Easter (excluding Sundays which are not fast days) with a somewhat unnecessary preparatory period of two and a half weeks from Septuagesima Sunday onwards. This period may have been included in the Lenten season because of the old order of fasting in the East in which Saturdays as well as Sundays were excluded from fasting, and the whole fast had to be completed before Holy Week, which was regarded as part of the festival of Easter. This is one of the many examples of the way in which the liturgical Calendar has grown through the ages rather than been planned.

The Ember Days, days of abstinence observed in the West on the Wednesdays, Fridays and Saturdays before the 2nd Sunday in Lent, Trinity Sunday, Michaelmas (29 September), and the fourth Sunday in Advent, may originally have been inaugurated in Rome about the third century to take the place of Italian agricultural festivals. An alternative theory, which seems more probable, is that they go back to ancient Jewish fasts (cf. Zechariah 8. 19 and the Dead Sea Scrolls). They are now regarded as days of prayer for the ministry preparatory to ordinations, which in the Roman Church always take place at these seasons.

Rogation Days, the three days before Ascension Day, began when Mamertus, Bishop of Vienne, (about 470) ordered special 'rogations' or litanies to be observed on these days at a time when the eruptions of the volcanoes of Auvergne were causing great distress in his diocese.

SAINTS' DAYS

The local remembrance of the *genethlion* (in Latin, *natale* = 'birthday') or day of the death of a martyr at his tomb goes back to the early second century. The classical instance of the beginning of such a cult is in the *Martyrdom of Polycarp*. After telling of his death by burning, the author, who was evidently an eye-witness, writes :

And so later we gathered up his bones, more precious than jewels, more valuable than gold, and laid them in a fitting place. There, when we assemble as we are able, the Lord will grant us to celebrate with gladness and joy the 'birthday' of the martyr, for the remembrance also of those who have already fought the fight [i.e., other martyrs] and for the discipline and preparation of those who will [be martyred] in the future.

Though this is a typical local cult, we see that it looks beyond the individual martyr who had belonged to the Church of Smyrna and commemorates martyrs in general. For several centuries even the calendars of Rome and other great sees retained a measure of this local character. Though in Jerusalem we find the beginning of a universal calendar in the commemoration of biblical saints, we must remember that Jerusalem of all places could claim them as *local* saints.

When it was desired to commemorate a saint other than one

who had died locally it was for some time thought necessary
to acquire some relic of him to be buried in front of the altar
of the church where the commemoration was to take place and
which might be dedicated in the saint's name. When the date
of a saint's death was unknown, his day was often fixed by
such a transference of relics or church dedication. E.g., the
joint festival of St. Peter and St. Paul on 29 June owes its
origin to the temporary removal of their remains from their
separate graves to a safer hiding place during the Decian
persecution; and the day of the Conversion of St. Paul, 25
January, owes its origin to the transference of some relic of
his to an unknown church in the South of France in the fifth
or sixth century. Such borrowings of saints paved the way for
a universal calendar. Byzantium, for instance, after it had
been renamed Constantinople and made the eastern capital
by Constantine, found itself without any notable local saints
and needed to supplement its meagre heritage by large-scale
borrowings. Later, when it was no longer considered necessary,
for the commemoration of a saint, to possess a relic of him,
the way was open for the provincial churches to adopt the
calendars of the great sees.

Obviously the ancient calandars of Christendom are
luxuriant growths which even those Churches of the Reformation that admit the commemoration of the saints and the
observance of other holy days would deem in need of radical
pruning. There is much to recommend a simplification in
which the Sundays of the year are all related to one or other
of the three major festivals of Christmas, Easter and Pentecost.
If saints are to be commemorated—and their remembrance
brings home to us the wonder of God's grace in human life
and declares to us our unity with the Church Triumphant—
our formation of a calendar might well follow the historical
development of early calendars, i.e., by our asking what great
men and women of God have passed into the folk memory of
the local Church, and then adding to their number a judicious
selection of names of those who have been universally acknow-

ledged to be saints. These would be for us the representatives of the universal Church. Above all, All Saints' Day reminds us that particular saints are only shining examples of the sanctity of the whole people of God all of whom are 'called to be saints'.

The Christian Calendar, as we have seen, emerged haphazard, and some of the motives operative in its development are best passed over. But, taken as a whole, it is the splendid fulfilment of the Church's urge to sanctify both time and life in submission to God's rule. If it is followed in worship and preaching by using a lectionary based upon it, it enables the minister to obey Paul's example of 'declaring the whole counsel of God' to his people instead of returning again and again to his own pet themes and scriptural passages and giving his people only some aspects of the Christian message. The consecration of life of which it is the declaration has been sublimely expressed in Latin verse by the Spanish poet, Prudentius :

This must be my message : 'O man, whoever thou art,
Thy mind has lost the world which it worshipped.
These things which it desired do not belong to God, to
  whom thou shalt belong.
At least under the shadow of death
Let thy sinful soul renounce all folly.
Let thy voice praise God, as thy deeds can never do.
Let the whole day long resound with hymns,
And no night pass without the worship of the Lord.
Let thy soul resist heresies and expound the catholic faith,
Trample on the rites of the heathen
And bring ruin, Rome, upon thine idols.
Let thy song be a tribute to the martyrs and praise to the
  apostles.'
While thus I write or proclaim,
May I be gloriously freed from the bonds of bodily life
By Him whose name my tongue shall utter at the last.

CHAPTER 10

WORSHIP ROOTED IN LIFE[1]

In the year 1932 Bishop Azariah of Dornakal, with the approval of the Episcopal Synod of his Church, published in Telugu a marriage service for use in his diocese. In it the essential Christian act of solemnization of matrimony was enriched with local marriage customs from non-Christian sources, where these were considered free from idolatrous associations. Demands that worship in India and other countries should be less foreign and more 'indigenous' were then of comparatively recent origin, and judging by the comment made on this service by the Episcopal Synod,[2] it was evidently hailed as a bold and enlightened step in the right direction.

It was particularly valuable and indeed urgent to begin this Indianization at the point of marriage. The dramatic poverty of our marriage service of Western origin constitutes in itself an additional temptation to those already tempted to contract mixed marriages by non-Christian rites. Perhaps even more cogent to Christians is the immensely powerful dramatic emphasis in Hindu marriage ceremonies on the binding and life-long character of the marriage vows. The tying together of the bride's and bridegroom's clothes, the binding together

---

[1] Reprinted from the *Indian Journal of Theology* (where it appeared under the title, 'The Indian Church at Worship') with the kind permission of the Editor. This Chapter is included in this book to emphasize that any study of worship must be made from a local standpoint which, in the case of the author, has for the past nineteen years been that of India. Also any embodiment of the age-long and world-wide heritage of the Church's worship must have its roots in the soil of the country where that embodiment takes place. Readers of the *International Review of Missions* during the past decade will be aware that similar thought and experiment has been taking place in many parts of Asia and Africa.

[2] See *Principles of Prayer Book Revision* (London, S.P.C.K., 1957), pp. 78f.

of their hands, the exchange of garlands, the seven steps walked together and the vow of which the sacredness is enhanced by its being made in the presence of fire—all these are a colourful Indian heritage. In view of the fact that marriage was a divine ordinance 'in the beginning' and Christ only endorsed what was already part of the basic structure of society, the Christian need have no hesitation in 'baptizing' this heritage to be part of the marriage rites of the Church.

Such may well have been the hopes entertained of this service; but nineteen years later, when enquiry was made about its use, the reply received from Bishop Azariah's successor was : 'Apparently only lip-service was paid in the matter of the use of this service. I can find little trace of its being used except occasionally in Dornakal itself.'[1] Such was the fate of a hopeful experiment, even though backed by the authority and forcefulness of that great bishop. It is not surprising that other experiments of this nature have come up against apathy and conservatism and met either with failure or only very limited success. With regard to marriage the best we can do to console ourselves is to reflect that the use in many parts of India of the *mangalasutra*[2] instead of the Western ring is a purely Indian custom. Here local tradition has gloriously triumphed. The Liturgy Committee of the Church of South India has been examining existing marriage rites and has recently published a C.S.I. rite designed to embody the principles which Bishop Azariah had in mind.[3] Perhaps today with the growing consciousness that the Church in India should give expression to its own heritage, the new experiment will be better received than that of a generation ago.

This instance we have described as typical of the reception

[1] Ibid., p. 79.

[2] A token which is worn on a thread round the neck : the tying of the thread by the bridegroom corresponds to the placing of the ring on the bride's finger.

[3] The Church of South India *Marriage Service* (O.U.P., 1960).

with which Indianizing of worship is inclined to meet must prompt us to reflect and to examine what it is we aim at doing when we set before ourselves the project of making Indian Christian worship 'more Indian'. The Creed in which we express our belief in 'the holy catholic Church' should remind us in our worship of Paul's great affirmation that 'there cannot be Greek and Jew, circumcision or uncircumcision, barbarian, Scythian, bondman, freeman : but Christ is all in all.' The Indian Church, therefore, can never be merely Indian : its members are heirs of the universal Church throughout the ages, whose heritage of worship we have been studying. The creative periods in worship, both that of the early centuries and that of the Reformation, had their main centres in other lands and their fruits have been brought to India by foreigners. Christians in India need not be embarrassed by this : it is part of their universal fellowship in Christ.

At the same time, as Dr. Sundkler in his book, *The Church of South India,* has pointed out, a law of the science of botany has its analogy in the subject we are studying : 'transplantation' has brought about a measure of 'mutation'. We have seen this in our study of the worship of the Christians of St. Thomas. They call themselves and are known by others as 'Syrians', and this is a recognition of the fact of their ancient connexions with the Churches of East and West Syria. In worship their rites have been imported from these regions; and yet when planted and rooted in India they have undergone some independent development, and Indian Christians have through the ages given to them a character which they can call their own.

The new formulations of worship which had their births at the Reformation have been brought to India by evangelists of many different denominations and often present a confused scene. They are of more recent transplantation and bear in a more marked degree the characteristics of the countries of their own origin. Also when the pioneer missionaries of these Churches came to India, it was hardly to be expected that the

simple, illiterate folk who formed the majority of their converts should make very much contribution of their own to the
development of Christian worship. Nor did the missionaries
themselves know enough about Indian art and culture, Indian
social and religious customs to be able to distil from them
elements that could enrich the Church's heritage of worship.
They were inclined to dismiss all these as belonging to the
darkness of pagan superstition and therefore to be wholly
abandoned at the renunciation by the convert in Baptism of
the devil and all his works. Converts too were sincere in their
desire to imitate in all things their fathers-in-God who had
brought them from darkness to light. Hence the prevalence
of Western forms of worship in our services, of Western
architecture in our churches and, in spite of many hopeful
developments in Indian church music, the prevalence in many
congregations of translations of Western hymns in Western
metre and set to Western hymn-tunes.

We must not go to the extreme of saying that this is all
wrong. As we have already affirmed, the Church transcends
national boundaries, and to use, for instance, a Hindi translation of a Lutheran or Anglican prayer book enables the Hindi-
speaking Christian to enter in a measure into its supra-national
heritage. Even the revised eucharistic rites of the Lutherans,
the Anglicans and the Church of South India have for the
most part only been 'Indianized' to the extent of including
some elements from the Syrian rites. The specifically Indian
contribution to their wording and structure is very small,
though the significance of these three largely independent
revisions, as having with remarkable accord returned to the
Church's classical heritage in worship, may be very great in
the future. We must not fail to mention the 'Indian Liturgy'
of the Church of India, Pakistan, Burma and Ceylon, which
is more thoroughgoing in its return to the Syrian heritage both
in wording and in the use of Syrian chants. But this liturgy is
only used in a few Marathi- and Malayalam-speaking congregations; and when we reflect that the Liturgy of St. James

is a comparatively recent importation into India, we must admit that the use of passages from it can hardly claim to be more Indian than the continued use of Anglican or Lutheran prayer books.

Similarly a case could be made for Western types of church architecture as better suited than that of Hindu temples or Muslim mosques to the essentially congregational character of Christian worship. Above all one would not wish to deprive the Indian Church entirely of the universal heritage of Western hymnody. Nor can it be said that a congregation which follows in the main a Western mode of worship merely imitates the West. As with the ancient Indian Syrian tradition, Protestant Christians in India have succeeded in giving to their more recently imported ways of worship a stamp of their own. Transplantation has indeed engendered mutation.

At the same time, we dare not be complacent and say that all is right. Worship, it has become a commonplace to say, must be related to the whole of life. Can we claim that Indian Christian worship, as it is at present conducted in most churches, is calculated to bring the treasures of Indian common life to the throne of grace? The vision of the glory of the nations being brought as tribute to Christ in his Kingdom must be our primary inspiration in seeking to make our worship a fitting expression of India's heritage. No less a reason will suffice. But a further consideration can only come second to this in importance. It is one of a more practical nature connected with the outreach of the Church's mission. What, we must ask, is the evangelistic value of our present ways of worship? To say that the normal worship of the Church is for instructed Christians and that it does not matter if a Hindu thinks it strange or foreign is not enough. The new convert, when he comes to church for the first time, will inevitably find some things strange and new to him; but in the main he ought to feel that the service in which he is taking part is something which could soon belong to him and to which he could soon belong. Can this be said of many of our

Christian services? If not, the value of all efforts to make the Indian Church's worship more Indian cannot be overstressed.

Let us start with music and poetry. Though translations of Western hymns have often been the foundation of an Indian Christian's personal devotion, the Westerner who hears them sung in church seldom feels that the singing of choir or congregation has come alive. It is significant too that hardly any new compositions in this mode, or even good translations, have been produced by Indians themselves. For a congregation to rely entirely on Western hymns is to live on borrowed capital and to prefer foreign servitude to native freedom.

The spirit, on the other hand, in which lyrics are sung to Indian music is entirely different. There can be no question that this singing is alive. And, more hopeful still, it is a heritage which is ever increasing. Never a Christmas passes without a new lyrical carol being composed, and if a lyric is required for worship on some special occasion, there is always a poet to write it and a musician to give it a tune. Indeed the compositions in our standard lyric books are only a tenth of this magnificent heritage of Christian folk-song, as those who are acquainted with the many unofficial collections of such lyrics in any one language will know. When also will our congregations of Anglican heritage realize that their painful efforts to fit their Psalms and Canticles to Western chants for which their language is unsuited is quite unnecessary when they are so much better sung in lyrical versions to Indian music?

Together with these lyrics which are sung in our services we must class the less formal sacred concert (*kalaksheba* or *bajna*) which is one of the best methods of educating our village congregations in the great themes and personalities of the Bible and is still more effective in its use as 'lyrical evangelism' directed to the non-Christian. Perhaps the Church in Andhra, where the people are gifted with a musical talent above that of many other areas, may claim to have advanced furthest in the use of their own Telugu poetry and Carnatic music, particularly at the great Christian conventions which take place in the month of May. In passing we may say that there is nothing more characteristic of India's religious pilgrimage than the *mela* or *jatra* and among Christians no type of meeting is more lastingly popular. In Palamcottah, Tirunelveli District, an occasion of this type was started over half a century ago by missionaries as a counter-attraction in the month of July to a popular Hindu festival. It is still celebrated with the same enthusiasm and to attend it is to meet the rural Church in all its vigour.

Western rites too can be given a more Indian form by the use of Indian music for versicles and responses, by singing lyrical versions of confessions, thanksgivings, the Creed and the Lord's Prayer, and by chanting lessons and prayers in the way that the *Vedas* are chanted. At Tamilnad Theological College we have experimented with this way of rendering Morning and Evening Prayer and with Carnatic settings to the congregational parts of the C.S.I. *Order for the Lord's Supper,* and similar ventures have been made in Jaffna, Ceylon and elsewhere.

Experiments in the use of Indian architectural themes in churches have been fewer; though many recent buildings have to a greater or lesser extent embodied some features of local architecture and carving. Bishop Azariah's inspired blending of architectural styles is an outstanding example to be followed (according to the spirit rather than the letter). Together with its Indo-saracenic dome and other features of Muslim architecture it has Dravidian pillars with their datura leaf–banana bud capitals—an effective symbolism of life out of death. Over all are a structure and proportions reminiscent of the renaissance architecture of St. George's Cathedral, Madras; so that in this splendid church East meets West. The use of the Indo-saracenic style might not be so well in place anywhere less close to a Muslim centre like Hyderabad, just as Dravidian pillars would not be appropriate to Delhi or Agra. The great buildings of St. John's College, Agra, including the chapel, are rightly of pure Indo-saracenic and might have been transported from Fatehpur Sikri, except for the cross that surmounts the main dome.

On the other hand, the chapel of the Christu-kulu Ashram, Tirupathur, is equally appropriate to its surroundings in its pure Dravidian, indistinguishable from the architecture of a South Indian Hindu temple, until you get near enough to see that all the symbolism is emphatically Christian. A less ambitious instance of an experiment in combining the two great architectural styles of India is worth recording, particularly as the village of Oyyangudi, where the building in question is situated, is somewhat off the beaten track in Tinnevelly District and not likely to be visited by many sightseers. In 1939 the Christian congregation there had collected enough money to build themselves a larger church and came to an architect with a request for a design for the new church. He firmly refused to design them one in pseudo-Gothic, which was what they had in mind, but persuaded them to accept a design which, though not Gothic, would satisfy the conservative villager by conforming to his notion of what a church should look like. The result was a building of the general shape and plan which we expect to find in a church, a shape which has been hallowed by centuries of use in Christian worship, and which declares the congregational character of that worship. This traditional appearance was enhanced by the retention of the fine tower of the old church, the design of which had been inspired by the tower of some English parish church. But though the windows and interior arches were pointed, as in Gothic, anyone who knew anything about architecture would recognize them as inspired by the Indo-saracenic form. And they were set on sturdy Dravidian pillars of single stone blocks carved with Christian symbols. This blending of the styles has a felicity and inspiration of its own; but except where an architect has been given the opportunity of experimenting in this way himself, such a line of architectural development has seldom been followed in the locality by the mason-architects of village churches. Another instance, we may say, of hide-bound conservatism such as Bishop Azariah's marriage service came up against. It is only fair to add that the bishop's architectural vision in Dornakal cathedral has inspired some imitation in neighbouring churches.

And may we plead that church furnishings should not be imported or copied from the West, but that Indian types of lamps, for instance, should be used instead of Western candlesticks? And should not we insist on the ancient oriental symbol of reverence, the removing of shoes before entering church? Should we not refuse also to allow our churches to be cluttered with ugly pews? To sit cross-legged on the floor is a posture which inspires greater reverence, as those who are accustomed to it well know.

We have already mentioned the Christian *jatra* as characteristically Indian. It is worth specifying two particular forms of it which generally have a more local character in their celebration. Firstly there is the home festival with its procession of prayer at every house and its lamp-lighting ceremony with the accompanying promise of faithfulness to marriage vows and mutual love in the home. This surely meets a need in India's society and the Church's contribution to it in an age when the whole structure of family life is undergoing transformation at the impact of modern technological developments. Finally there is the long-established and ever-popular harvest festival which gives expression to what is common to all Indian devotion, Christian and non-Christian, the desire to offer the fruits of the earth to God. No one who has attended a village harvest festival can say that the Church in India has not made a significant contribution to world-wide worship here. In the long processions of men, women and children bringing up their baskets of grain and fruit, their chickens and their goats, we see a symbol of the end of all true worship, the offering of man's daily life and its products to God that he may sanctify them for the fulfilment of his purpose of the salvation of mankind.

A SHORT LIST OF BOOKS FOR FURTHER STUDY

Baumstark, A. *Comparative Liturgy* (English ed. by F. L. Cross, London, 1958)

Benoit, J. D. *Liturgical Renewal: Catholic and Protestant Developments on the Continent* (trans. Hudson; London, 1958)

Bouyer, L. *Life and Liturgy* (London, 1956)

Brightman, F. E. *Liturgies Eastern and Western*, Vol. I, *Eastern Liturgies* (Oxford, 1896)

„ *The English Rite* (London, 1915)

Brilioth, Y. *Eucharistic Faith and Practice, Evangelical and Catholic* (trans. Hebert, London, 1930)

Brown, L. W. *The Indian Christians of St. Thomas* (Cambridge, 1956)

Clarke, W. K. Lowther (editor). *Liturgy and Worship* (London, 1932)

Cullmann, O. *Baptism in the New Testament* (London, 1950)

„ *Early Christian Worship* (London, 1953)

„ and Leenhardt, J. *Essays on the Lord's Supper* (London, 1950)

Daniélou, J. *The Bible and Liturgy* (London, 1960).

Davies, J. G. *An Experimental Liturgy* (London, 1959)

Dix, G. *The Apostolic Tradition of St. Hippolytus* (London, 1937)

„ *The Shape of the Liturgy* (London, 1946)

Dugmore, C. W. *The Mass and the English Reformers* (London, 1958)

Edwall, P., and others. *Ways of Worship* (London, S.C.M. Press, 1951)[1]

Flemington, W. F. *The New Testament Doctrine of Baptism* (London, 1948)

Garrett, T. S. *The Liturgy of the Church of South India* (Madras and London, 2nd ed., 1954)

„ *Worship in the Church of South India* (London, 1958)

Grisbrooke, W. J. *Anglican Liturgies of the Seventeenth and Eighteenth Centuries* (London, 1959)

Herbert, A. S. *Worship in Ancient Israel* (London, 1959)

Higgins, A. J. B. *The Lord's Supper in the New Testament* (London, 1952)

Jeremias, J. *The Eucharistic Words of Jesus* (trans. Ehrhardt; Oxford (Blackwell), 1955)

Jungmann, J. A. *The Mass of the Roman Rite* (trans. of *Missarum Solemnia: eine genetische Erklärung der Römische Messe;* London (slightly abridged, 1 vol. ed.), 1959; complete ed. (2 vols.) New York (Benziger), 1951-55)

„ *The Early Liturgy to the Time of Gregory the Great* (London, 1960).

Jungmann, J. A. *Public Worship* (London, Challoner Pubns., 1951)

Lampe, G. W. H. *The Seal of the Spirit* (London, 1951)

Maxwell, W. D. *An Outline of Christian Worship* (London, 1936, reprinted with corrections, 1945)

„   *A History of Worship in the Church of Scotland* (London, 1955)

McArthur, A. A. *The Evolution of the Christian Year* (London, 1953)

Micklem, N. (editor) *Christian Worship* (Oxford, 1936)

Moule, C. F. D. *Worship in the New Testament* (London 1961)

Nicholls, W. *Jacob's Ladder: The Meaning of Worship* (London, 1958)

Oakley, A. *The Orthodox Liturgy* (London, 1958)

Oesterley, W. O. E. *The Jewish Background of the Christian Liturgy* (Oxford, 1925)

Pius XII. *Mediator Dei* (Encyclical, Eng. trans. published by Catholic Truth Society, London, 1947)

Porter, W. S. *The Gallican Rite* (London, 1958)

Shands, A. R. *The Liturgical Movement and the Local Church* (London, 1959)

Srawley, J. H. *The Early History of the Liturgy* (Cambridge, 2nd ed., 1947)

„   *The Liturgical Movement* (London, 1954)

Thurian, M. *Confession* (trans. Hudson; London, 1958)

Underhill, E. *Worship* (London, 1936)

1 See also footnote on p. 76.

INDEX

N

Set in Great Britain by
Foundry Press Ltd.,
and reprinted lithographically by
The Curwen Press Ltd.,
London